PROMOTING INDEPENDENT LEARNING IN THE PRIMARY CLASSROOM

Enriching the primary curriculum: child, teacher, context

Series editor: Janet R. Moyles

This series highlights some of the major challenges and issues which face teachers on a day-to-day basis in handling their apparently ever widening roles in primary schools. Curriculum experiences can, and should, be enriching and stimulating for everyone but there must be a recognition and appreciation of the crucial interface between child, teacher and the context of school and society, rather than a focus on mere curriculum 'delivery'.

Each volume in the series seeks to enrich and extend readers' curriculum thinking beyond the current narrow confines through recognizing and celebrating the very essence of what makes primary teaching demanding but exciting, creative, dynamic and, yes, even enjoyable! The series recognizes that at the heart of teaching lies children and that 'subjects' are merely tools towards enabling an education which develops both understanding and enthusiasm for life-long learning.

The authors' underpinning, integrated rationale is to enable teachers to analyse their own practices by exploring those of others through cameos of real life events taken from classroom and school contexts. The aim throughout is to help teachers regain their sense of ownership over changes to classroom and curricular practices and to develop an enhanced and enriched understanding of theory through practice.

Current and forthcoming titles:

Florence Beetlestone: *Creative children, imaginative teaching*
Max de Boo: *Enquiring children, challenging teaching*
Deirdre Cook and Helen Finlayson: *Interactive children, communicative teaching*
Patricia Maude: *Physical children, active teaching*
Roger Merry: *Successful children, successful teaching*
Wendy Suschitzky and Joy Chapman: *Valued children, informed teaching*
Jill Williams: *Promoting Independent Learning in the Primary Classroom*

PROMOTING INDEPENDENT LEARNING IN THE PRIMARY CLASSROOM

Jill Williams

Open University Press
Buckingham · Philadelphia

Open University Press
Celtic Court
22 Ballmoor
Buckingham
MK18 1XW

email: enquiries@openup.co.uk
world wide web: www.openup.co.uk

and
325 Chestnut Street
Philadelphia, PA 19106, USA

First Published 2003

A catalogue record of this book is available from the British Library

ISBN   0 335 20016 8 (pb)   0 335 20017 6 (hb)

Library of Congress Cataloging-in-Publication Data
Williams, Jill, 1942-
    Promoting independent learning in the primary classroom /
Jill Williams.
        p. cm. – (Enriching the primary curriculum–child, teacher,
    context)
    Includes bibliographical references and index.
    ISBN 0-335-20017-6 – ISBN 0-335-20016-8 (pbk.)
    1. Independent study–Great Britain.   2. Education,
Elementary–Great Britain.   I. Title.   II. Series.

    LB1601.3.W55 2003
    372.139′4–dc21

                                                        2002074970

Typeset by Graphicraft Limited, Hong Kong
Printed in Great Britain by Biddles Limited, www.biddles.co.uk

Contents

Series editor's preface

Cameo

Glenn has taught across the age range in different primary schools for the last 15 years, specializing in art. In that time, he has had to make many adjustments in his thinking. The emphasis now appears to have shifted significantly from considering the learning needs of children as paramount, to 'delivering' a curriculum over which he feels little ownership and about which he feels even less real enthusiasm! The National Curriculum, with its individual subjects and language of 'teaching', not to mention an impending Office for Standards in Education (Ofsted) inspection, has shaken his confidence somewhat in his own understanding of what primary education is all about. It has also meant that he feels *he* is doing most of the learning, rather than the children – all those detailed plans and topic packs for individual subjects which teachers have been developing within the school seem to Glenn to leave little for children to actually do except explore the occasional artefact and fill in work sheets.

Yet he knows that he enjoys the 'buzz' of teaching, revels in being part of children's progress and achievements, delights in those rare times when he can indulge in art activities with children, is appreciated by parents and colleagues for the quality of his work and, generally, still finds his real heart lies in being an educator and doing something worthwhile. His constant question to himself is 'How can I work with children in ways I feel and *know* are appropriate and yet meet the outside demands made on me?'

Sound familiar? You may well begin to recognize a 'Glenn' within you! He encapsulates the way many teachers are feeling at the present time and the persistent doubts and uncertainties which continually underpin many teachers' work. In the early and middle years of primary schooling in particular, teachers are facing great challenges in conceiving how best to accommodate the learning needs of children in a context of growing pressure, innovation and subject curriculum demand. Yet conscientiousness drives the professional to strive for greater understanding – that little bit more knowledge or skill might just make a big difference to one child, or it might provide improved insights into one aspect of the curriculum.

Glenn, like many teachers, needs time, encouragement and support to reflect on his current practice and to consider in an objective way the changes needed. Rather than trying to add something else to an already overcrowded curriculum, today's teachers should consider those existing aspects which are fundamental to ensuring that children are not only schooled but educated in the broadest possible sense. Only then can we begin to sort out those things which are vital, those things we would like to do, and those things which would benefit from a rethink.

This series aims to offer practitioners food for thought as well as practical and theoretical support in establishing, defining and refining their own understandings and beliefs. It focuses particularly on enriching curriculum experiences for everyone through recognizing and appreciating the crucial interface between the child, the teacher and the context of primary education, including the curriculum context. Each title in the series seeks collectively and individually to enhance teachers' understanding about the theories which underpin, guide and enrich quality practice in a range of broader curriculum aspects, while acknowledging issues such as class size and overload, common across primary schools today.

Each book operates from the basis of exploring teachers' sound – frequently intuitive – experiences and understanding of teaching and learning processes and outcomes which most teachers inevitably possess in good measure and which, like Glenn, they often feel constrained to use. For example, the editor is regularly told by teachers and others in primary schools that they 'know' or 'feel' that play for children is or must be a valuable process, yet they are also aware that this is not often reflected in their planning or curriculum management and that the context of education generally is antithetical to play. What is more, they really do not know what to do about it and find articulating the justification for play practices extremely difficult. Other writers in the series have suggested that this is also the case in their areas of expertise.

All the books in this series seek to enrich and extend teachers' curriculum thinking beyond the level of just 'subjects', into dimensions related to the teaching and learning needs of children and the contextual demands faced by schools. The books cover areas such as creativity, success and competence, exploration and problem solving, information technology across subjects and boundaries, play in the primary curriculum, questioning and teacher–child interactions, values in relation to equality issues, social, moral and spiritual frameworks, and physical aspects of teaching and learning. Each book has had, within its working title, the rationale of the unique triad of child, teacher and context which underpins all primary schooling and education, for example in this particular case, creative children and imaginative teaching. This structure serves to emphasize for authors the inextricable and imperative balance in this triad for effective classroom and curriculum practices. The model we have developed and agreed is shown in Figure 1.

All the writers in the series have been concerned to emphasize the quality, nature and extent of existing classroom practices, and how it is possible to build on these sound pedagogical bases. For this reason, chapters within each title often begin with two or

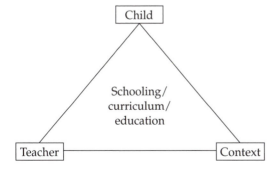

Figure 1 Child, teacher, context

more cameos offering features of practice as starting points for teasing out aspects requiring enquiry, analysis, evaluation and discussion. Chapters then develop their own relevant themes but with consistent reference to what these mean to children and teachers within the general autonomy, and constraints, of the school context.

Issues concerning the *child* take their stance from cognitive psychology (as this book does) and include the child as:

- an active searcher after meaning;
- an individual with particular perceptions of the world and their part in it;
- a person who can reflect on their own learning and understanding;
- a learner with his or her own curriculum needs and interests to be considered;
- an interactive person, learning in collaboration with peers and adults;
- a unique individual but also one with collective needs;
- a member of a 'social' community, i.e. home, family, school, wider community.

Aspects to do with the teaching role lay stress on the *teacher* as a reflective and critical professional who will occasionally but regularly need to stand back from day-to-day practice in order to think about and analyse the triadic relationships and to acknowledge:

- their own learning styles and experiences;
- their own beliefs, values, knowledge and conceptual understanding of pedagogy;
- their need to raise questions about practice and find solutions in an ongoing way;
- their role as mutual learners with children and colleagues;
- their responsibilities as facilitators of learning, as models of learning and as negotiators of meaning with children;
- their role in enabling children's learning rather than always in 'teaching';
- their function as observers and assessors of children's understandings as well as outcomes;
- their obligation clearly to conceptualize the whole curriculum of which the National Curriculum is a part.

When we consider the *context* of pedagogy, this focus subsumes such aspects as the learning environment, school ethos and the actual classroom and school. It also includes such elements as:

- the physical environment – indoors and outdoors;
- the social environment of school and schooling (e.g. is the child an outcome of the context or has the context influenced the child?);
- the psychological environment of school and schooling;
- the philosophical considerations within schools and aspects such as teachers' beliefs and values;
- the curriculum context, including the National Curriculum where this is relevant and appropriate, but also showing where this does not necessarily meet pedagogical needs;
- the frameworks within which the whole concept of schooling takes place and where this fits education in a broader sense.

The overall rationale for each book in the series starts from a belief that teachers should be enabled to analyse their own practices in specific aspects of the broader curriculum as a major aspect of their professionalism. The books are particularly useful at a time of continual curriculum change, when reflection is being focused back upon the child and pedagogy generally as the only perpetuating and consistent elements.

As an integral component, all the books weave teachers' assessment of children's learning and understanding into each particular focus, the intention being to show how the planning >learning>assessment>planning cycle is vital to the quality and success of children's and teachers' learning experiences. With their practical ideas, challenges and direct relevance to classroom practice, these books offer ways of establishing theory as *the* adjunct to practice; they build on teachers' thinking about how they already work in the classroom and help teachers to consider how they may enrich, extend and advance their practices to the mutual benefit of themselves, the children, the curriculum and education in society as a whole.

Promoting Independent Learning in the Primary Classroom sets out to explore how independence in children can be promoted (or otherwise!) in early years and primary classrooms. Jill Williams bases much of her writing in the book on empirical research evidence from classrooms and other settings in different parts of the world. This has led her to the view that independent children work to higher standards, are better motivated and have higher self-esteem, something to which we all, as early years and primary teachers, definitely aspire. If for no other reason, this makes independence an imperative for education today.

Over the last few years, increasing government prescription has marched its way into primary teachers' lives either from the National Curriculum or from the National Literacy and Numeracy Strategies. Prescription for teachers has impacted upon them in many ways, not least the feeling that children's activities need to be equally closely prescribed. In out-of-school life, concerns for children's safety have also meant reduced levels of independence. Yet, conversely, industry bemoans the lack of independent thinking amongst school leavers.

It has always struck me that we seem in the UK to work hard with young children to encourage independence yet then successively take it away from them as they progress through primary and finally into secondary schools, then try to give it back to them again at University level! In primary education, we speak the language of children being 'independent' – encouraging them to think for themselves, make judgements, solve problems and so on – then require them to follow a curricular regime which is based on an input/output model which can leave little time for independent thinking or action. Close adult direction of every learning experience, can leave children feeling very disempowered and make dependence on the teacher a necessity. Yet as Jill Williams asserts 'being independent suggests being able to do things for oneself' and act autonomously. But ensuring effective curriculum provision that is supported by meaningful and relevant learning experiences for children can be extremely challenging for teachers.

In the six main chapters of the book, Jill guides her readers through a series of discussions about a range of aspects to do with independence such as the relationship between the rhetoric of independence and the classroom reality. In the following chapters, communication and independence, motivation and ownership, the implications of environment for independence, the potential for change in practices and finally her views on how the newly revived 'topic approach' in primary, are all explored thoroughly. As with all the books in the series, all the chapters are supported by reference to informative research and theories of others, and the issues are brought to life for readers through cameos of learning and teaching, the concepts from which help formulate the ideas weaving through each chapter.

Jill makes it clear to teachers that allowing children to be independent can be antithetical to their own pragmatic needs within the classroom for a certain level of conformity. She asks teachers to question whether they want children who can make their own independent decisions or children who can merely 'get on' and 'keep out of the teacher's hair'? True independent pedagogy requires teachers to acknowledge the children's potential for responsibility: even the youngest children can operate in ways which challenge them cognitively, through play and other activities, without continual adult intervention. Similarly, independence is not a fixed factor but operates at varying levels for different individuals: this means trusting children to respond in relevant ways but also acknowledging that this may sometimes challenge teachers and other adults!

This vital book is to be highly commended for approaching a philosophical concept about which much is said but little definitive is written that can support teachers and other practitioners in exploring the issues for themselves and the children with whom they work. Schools have a responsibility in this era to instil in children the ability to think for themselves and to make decisions based on clear and well thought-through analyses of needs: these are vital skills for the twenty-first century. However, such skills need to be taught, developed and encouraged through the education system, especially for 3–11-year-olds. This is part of growing up and learning both to respect others and also to trust oneself. Never has the topic been so necessary as now. Here is a text to encourage and persuade readers to restore at least something of children's independence through their classroom practices and ultimately through small but significant changes to teachers' own thinking.

Janet Moyles

Acknowledgements

Writing this book has allowed me to talk to teachers and children and to try to understand how an independent and creative approach to teaching and learning must be a part of the education of the future generation. I would like to thank them all for the time that they have taken to discuss their viewpoints and the welcome that I was given in their classrooms. My particular thanks must go to the series editor, Janet Moyles, who has waited patiently for copy and given her time generously to support and encourage the completion of the text. My husband Reg has been quietly supportive and allowed us to forego a long summer holiday to allow me time to read and to write. Finally, thanks go to my university colleague Mary Chilcott who has supported me in a variety of ways and introduced me to skills and techniques that helped to bring the manuscript to its conclusion.

Introduction

Independent approaches to teaching and learning should have mutual benefits for children and teachers. In this book independence and its relationship with responsibility, autonomy and creativity is illustrated with cameos of children's experiences, as well as through case studies and observations. In writing this book I have worked closely with a survey group of eight teachers. Whilst they all emphasized the importance of an independent climate for learning, some saw constraints on encouraging independence. Some teachers realized that it was their own pedagogical insecurity that caused them to tighten their control over children and narrow their opportunities for individual thought and action. The teachers' positive views, as well as their uncertainties, provide a framework for discussion in the chapters that follow.

Bruner (1996: 64) sets a challenge for teachers to rethink pedagogy and modify conventional and often restrictive classroom practice.

> Modern pedagogy is moving increasingly to the view that the child should be aware of her own thought processes, and that it is crucial for the pedagogical theorist and teacher alike to help her to become more meta-cognitive, to be as aware of how she goes about learning and thinking as she is about the subject matter she is studying.

Independence, responsibility and autonomy

Independence

Being independent suggests being able to do things for oneself. An increase in independent attitudes and skills is a sign of growing up. Children growing up in western societies are applauded when they walk, talk, feed and make complex choices. Trevarthen (2000) uses the term *intersubjectivity* to describe the synchrony of gestures and vocalization between mother and baby, where the infant is both able to lead the interaction and to respond accordingly.

Further development of independence relies on the attitudes and influences prevailing in the home environment. Some academics believe that children are increasingly overprotected (Furedi 2001). Whilst many children no longer have opportunities for experimentation, risk taking or adventure, others will have had a range of independent and challenging experiences. On entry to school, most children will be motivated to learn and some will be more eager than others to demonstrate their independence. Teachers need to appreciate the range of attitudes and experience that children bring with them to school and to provide a climate in which children can reach their individual potential and where an increase in independence, as well as collective responsibility, is valued.

Responsibility

Responsibility is closely related to independence. Children experience independence and develop knowledge and skills before taking responsibility. Responsibility, like independence, is culturally determined. Children may be given limited responsibility for cleaning out a guinea pig's cage or continuing responsibility for the management of younger siblings. In many cultures independence and responsibility will relate directly to survival. In Northern Thailand, the Hmong children have responsibility for bush knives from an early age. They are preparing for their role as hunters in the rain forest with practical experience of using tools for a range of tasks. These independent, responsible children are dependent on mastering a range of skills that will contribute to the survival of their group.

Figure I.1 In northern Thailand, the Hmong children have responsibility for bush knives from an early age

Autonomy

In the National Curriculum there is a requirement that schools should 'influence and reflect the values of society' and '... develop pupils' integrity and autonomy...' (DfEE/QCA 1999: 11). Autonomy is variously described as personal freedom, freedom of the will, or the ability to make decisions about what to do rather than being told or being influenced by others. Can autonomy really be an option for young children and is autonomy necessarily desirable? If being autonomous involves being personally free then it is hard to see how it can be achieved in a school situation. In all societies humans achieve varying degrees of independence, followed by personal and collective responsibility, but an autonomous route may lead to a scant regard for the well-being of others. It seems from the quotation above that it is children's *integrity* that should be fostered, and indeed the National Curriculum requires children to respect their own culture and the culture of others and to be aware of different ways of doing things. It is important that differences, as well as similarities, are revealed and allowed to contribute to a classroom culture that supports children's rights to self-determination, self-respect and responsibility.

Independence and education

The attitude to independent learning has been considered in a range of government reports and research. The elementary education system in the UK, pre-1944, preserved the social order and prepared children for work (Alexander 1995). The Plowden Report (CACE 1967) heralded optimistic views of primary education and changes in curriculum focus and delivery. A developmentally appropriate educational stance was taken in which there was respect for individuals, equality of opportunity, and commitment to high standards. Educational debates followed, fuelled by largely unsubstantiated views of uncontrolled progressive ideas. Inauguration of 'The Great Debate,' by James Callaghan in 1976, together with research (Bennett 1976) and the ORACLE studies on primary teaching that took place between 1975 and 1983 highlighted concern over teaching the three Rs.

In 1985 the government report, *Better Schools* (DES 1985a), advocated building on children's enthusiasm, and making plain the link between pupils' educational experiences and the relevance they have for everyday life. Promotion of educational inquiry and a match between the nature of the work and the characteristics and stage of development of the pupils was advocated. *The Curriculum from 5 to 16* recommended an approach where '. . . sometimes pupils should carry considerable responsibility for deciding the direction of their work' (HMI 1985: 10). *A Framework for the Primary Curriculum* (NCC 1989a) and *A Curriculum for All* (NCC 1989b) were the first of a series of non-statutory guidance documents for the implementation of the National Curriculum. Good practice was seen as encouraging pupils' questioning, self-confidence, self-discipline and developing partnerships with teachers, which encourages active learning. *The Whole Curriculum*

(NCC 1990: 9) asked the question, 'Are they (the pupils) given responsibility for their own learning?' *Starting with Quality*, the Rumbold Report (DES 1990), considered the quality of experience for 3 to 4-year-olds. Importance was placed on the interrelationship between children's experiences and subsequent planning. Attitudes relating to learning were to include 'respect, tolerance, independence, perseverance and curiosity' (DES 1990: 36).

Alexander *et al.* (1992) challenged the notions of child-centred education and the legacy left by the Plowden Report. They considered a balance of teaching approaches, including giving more independence to children capable of working on their own, and avoiding neglecting children, or leaving them with books and inappropriate work cards. *Well-managed Classes* (Ofsted 1991) provided evidence from case studies of six teachers. Where children were taking responsibility; there was a shared approach to learning; activities were organized to demonstrate maturity and responsibility; and pupils had access to materials to enable them to complete tasks independently. Well-organized classrooms were seen as those where pupils had responsibility for materials and making choices. Groups were organized to give opportunities for leadership and responsibility and to allow children to work unsupervised when teachers were with another group (Ofsted 1993: 20). *Primary Matters* (Ofsted 1994), in discussing unsuccessful lessons, cited an over-reliance on work sheets. Effective teachers were seen to use questions effectively, assess children's knowledge and challenge their thinking. *Key Characteristics of Effective Schools* (Sammons *et al.* 1995) cited research that showed substantial gains in effectiveness when self-esteem is raised and children have an active role and share responsibility for their own learning. Throughout this ten-year period, responsibility, independence and active learning were generally viewed positively. The National Curriculum (DfEE/QCA 1999: 11) further requires the school curriculum to '. . . develop (pupils') confidence in their capacity to learn and work independently and collaboratively'. A welcome addition to documents supporting independence and creativity was the report from the National Advisory Committee on Creative and Cultural Education. It is suggested that a creative approach to teaching and learning involves providing 'opportunities for young people to explore and recognise what their own assumptions and values are and how they have been formed' (NACCCE 1999: 97).

Investigating independence

In researching this book, the author spent time in English schools talking with teachers and observing and documenting independent practice in classrooms. Cameos and case studies focus mainly on children's capabilities and on adult acceptance that children's determination, knowledge and understanding need to become a part of what Katz and Chard (1990) call the art of living. The cameos in this book are taken from primary classrooms and from the wider environment. There are 'exotic' examples with children using bush knives in Thailand and young girls with responsibility for small babies in Malawi. Views on independence and its place in the contemporary primary classroom came from informal discussions with 80 teachers. Themes include the meaning and benefits of independence in education; establishment and maintenance of independent environments; and external and internal pressures on encouraging independence.

Chapter 1 explores the rhetoric and reality of an independent approach to teaching and learning in schools. Chapter 2 looks at the relationship between effective communication and independence. Cameos and evidence of children's work include speaking and listening and writing. In Chapter 3 the development of children's intrinsic motivation and perseverance is shown to encourage independence and ownership. The link between home and school is seen to be important. Chapter 4 investigates influences on classroom management and organization, including the impact of the Literacy Hour. A framework is suggested for auditing the classroom environment. Chapter 5 presents 'independent classrooms' in practice. Elements of the Reggio Emilia and High/Scope teaching and learning frameworks provide inspiration for possible thoughtful classroom modifications. Chapter 6 proposes a positive view of teaching and learning through a topic approach and provides exciting evidence of children's independent and creative thinking.

A journey is just beginning to find out something of the reality of an independent approach to teaching and learning.

1

An independent approach to teaching and learning: rhetoric or reality?

Cameo 1

Three 11-year-old children enter a classroom, where 9-year-olds are working. The older children carry clipboards and move confidently to the teacher. Reece explains, 'We are helping to write the school prospectus and we want new children to know what people think about the school.' Samantha adds, 'When we went into Reception we asked the children to draw pictures of their favourite school thing.' The teacher explains the children's task to her class and asks for volunteers to be interviewed. Three hands go up and perceptive questioning follows.

Cameo 2

Darren, Aaron and Winston are 9 years old. They are constructing a bridge using newspaper and tape. They ascertain that strength from the paper can be achieved by twisting and joining. They make a variety of stable shapes and begin the structure with a picture of the Forth Bridge as a point of reference. At first they work systematically but soon they use the paper rolls as swords and stick the tape to one another. They lose interest in the task and the conversation turns to home experience.

Darren: I've got my own mini.
Winston: You can't drive a car 'til you're grown up.
Darren: My dad bought it. It was scrap. He rebuilt it and I helped him. We had to lift the engine out and I got greasy. I rubbed the body down with Dad. We

> sprayed it yellow. It's got my name on it. It's cool.
> When I can see out of the windscreen I can drive it.
> *Aaron:* My dad's got a 'banger' and he might let me help him.
> *Darren:* We've got land and I can drive when I reach the
> clutch. My brother's got a bike (motor bike).
> He's 10.

Cameo 3

8-year-old Flora is responsible for her 5-year-old sister Fanny and her 6-month-old brother Joseph. Flora's education is intermittent because of the long, steep descent from her village to the school on the shores of Lake Malawi in Central Africa. The children's mother pounds cassava, a poor quality root crop. Her husband died of an Aids-related illness during the previous year.

Introduction

This chapter considers the contribution that independence makes to children's education and questions whether an independent approach to teaching and learning can be a reality or simply rhetoric. I carried out research with 80 primary teachers (hereafter called 'the survey teachers'), discussing aspects of independence. The teachers considered issues such as:

- what is understood by independence for 4 to 11-year-old children;
- what effect an independent approach has on teaching and learning;
- how an environment that promotes independence and responsibility can be achieved;
- whether it is possible to promote and maintain an independent approach to teaching and learning.

Two distinct views on what is understood by independence are apparent from the teachers' responses. Independent children are either seen as being able to organize themselves and to seek help as necessary, or to work in isolation without recourse to others. This chapter and the chapters that follow consider these interpretations, as well as the responses to a variety of other issues.

The teacher

A problem for teachers is maintaining a sensitive respect for children's independent responses and personal and creative contributions, while at the same time ensuring that curriculum targets are met. Moyles (1992: 23) sees an important relationship between teachers' preferred teaching styles and their ability to 'learn from what happens in the classroom not just about the children, but about the children's contribution to the teaching and learning processes'. A teaching style that encourages a variety of contributions from children will be one that recognizes the importance of an independent approach to teaching and learning.

When working independently children behave differently from working under direction. Fisher (1996: 27) says that '. . . observations of children working alone usually reveal fresh perspectives on the children as learners'. Many children respond well to tackling tasks on their own, especially if they know that there are realistic expectations of them (Cook and Finlayson 1999). Following the survey, teachers' views on independence are reflected upon under tentative, thematic headings.

Independence for 4 to 11-year-old children

The survey reveals two distinct views of independence.

The first view presents independent children as those who are able to make decisions when they are:

- in control and able to make choices about possible directions for activities;
- respected for their ideas as well as valued for who they are;
- able to learn how to learn and how to think;
- given confidence to question, hypothesize and make decisions based on prior knowledge;
- able to function by themselves and also to be confident in seeking help and communicating with peers and adults;
- motivated to take risks in a supportive environment, to revisit tasks and to try again without pressure;
- able to work without always needing to seek approval;
- able to use their own initiative, make personal contributions and balance the expectations of others;

- responsible for helping to create, organize and maintain a learning environment;
- able to operate within the social framework of the class/school and to bring personal experience, creativity, imagination and self-expression to tasks.

These enthusiastic and positive responses contribute to a view of independence where motivated, enthusiastic children are given responsibility and are also encouraged to interact with peers and adults. The term *interactionist independence* is used to describe this view.

The second view of an independent attitude to teaching and learning considers independent children as able to:

- work on their own and think for themselves;
- perform tasks, both in and out of the classroom, without adult intervention;
- solve problems without reference to others.

These responses represent what has been termed *isolationist independence*. This relates to the view of independence presented in the National Literacy Strategy. The teachers who hold this view emphasize the need to *teach and practise* strategies for independence. This again is in line with the Literacy Strategy (DfEE 1998) where children should be trained to:

- listen;
- follow instructions;
- develop skills to further their learning;
- observe rules and work within them;
- know what steps to go through if in difficulty;
- use self-help strategies for spelling, research and accessing information;
- understand that they must not disturb the teacher.

It is useful at this point to summarize the two views of independence.

- An *interactionist* view, where children are motivated, good problem solvers, effective communicators and able to seek help as appropriate.
- An *isolationist* view, where children are trained to develop skills for self-sufficiency and to work alone.

The isolationist view of independence appears to be mechanistic and prescriptive. It denies motivated children the opportunity to acquire independent behaviour patterns through interaction and encouragement. With contemporary pressure to predetermine curriculum outcomes and to aim for specific targets, it is understandable that strategies that help with efficient time management and slick, conformist, behavioural responses will be viewed as expedient by some teachers. *Training* children to be independent may then seem, by teachers, to be expedient.

In a truly effective classroom, there must surely be a sensitive balance between the two views of independence provided by the survey teachers. Fisher (1996: 76) says that 'there are too many children in a class for a teacher to be able to teach all of them directly all the time'. Well-trained independent children will obviously alleviate pressure on these teachers but their independence should stem from motivation and personal pride and not simply in response to training.

Some responses also raise concerns about whether *all* children will experience an independent approach to teaching and learning. The following examples exemplify these concerns.

- Independent children are *able to operate within the social framework of the class.*

What about those children who have to make significant social adjustment to the school context?

- Independent children *make decisions based on prior knowledge.*

Will *prior knowledge* include knowledge gained from home experiences and will this knowledge always be considered relevant to school decisions?

Will *all* children be given opportunities to operate independently in classrooms?

The impact that independence has on teaching

Some teachers in the survey saw independent children allowing teachers a chance:

- to organize a wider range of activities, knowing that some children are independent;

- to focus on 'teaching' rather than on 'housekeeping', through being able to delegate tasks to those children who know how to achieve them;
- to do some direct teaching with other groups in the knowledge that they are released from the supervision of some group tasks;
- to hand over responsibility to some children.

From these responses there is again an indication that not *all* children will experience independence. Responses such as '. . . some children will have a degree of independence', and '. . . those children who know how to achieve [tasks]' indicates that independence is defined by the school culture and will not be an option for every child. Further discussion with the survey group showed that teachers valued the group of children on whom they could rely, because it allowed them to concentrate on 'less advantaged' children. Coulby (1995), however, when discussing behaviour management, suggests that *all* children should be given opportunities for responsibility and independence.

The next set of responses provides additional evidence for an *isolationist* view of independence.

Independent children allow teachers time to:

- concentrate on support work with specific children because independent children are less demanding;
- do more important things;
- work with individuals in the class.

An *isolationist* view of independence sits uncomfortably alongside an inquiry-based or social constructivist approach to learning. Such an approach places value on social situations for the promotion of effective learning (Ritchie and Ollerenshaw 1993; Ritchie 1995; Johnston 1996). The work of Vygotsky and Bruner stresses the importance of the social climate in which children learn and the importance of linguistic interaction between adults and children. De Boo (1999: 2) relates independence to learners who usually require 'cooperative behaviour and communication with others'. Bruner (1996) sees acquired knowledge as most useful to a learner when it is discovered through the learner's own cognitive efforts. It is then related to what has been learned previously.

Teachers and pedagogy

Alexander (2000: 540) describes pedagogy as encompassing 'the performance of teaching together with the theories, beliefs, policies and controversies that inform and shape it.' He says that '. . . pedagogy connects the apparently self-contained act of teaching with culture, structure and mechanisms of social control'. Working with pedagogy that respects the individual nature of learning is definitely important when there is a climate of pre-determined curriculum outcomes. Teachers have a professional responsibility to provide children with opportunities to '. . . build on strengths, interests and experiences . . .' (DfEE/QCA 2000: 12). Bruner (1996) sets a challenge for many teachers to rethink their pedagogy and to modify conventional and often restrictive classroom practice. National and local pressures may influence teachers' style of teaching but rational response to educational challenges should accommodate changes without disturbing sound foundations for learning.

The detailed subject content of the curriculum, specific targets and standardized tests are national requirements. Values and purposes that underpin the National Curriculum (DfEE/QCA 1999: 10) are concerned with reflecting 'the values of society and the kind of society we want it to be'. Schools should empathize with children and allow them to enjoy their environment in an atmosphere of friendship and respect (Coulby 2000). The Curriculum guidance for the foundation stage (DfEE/QCA 2000: 12) encourages flexible responses to the needs of children and provision of opportunities for children to explore, experiment, plan and make decisions for themselves with resources that inspire them: 'The school curriculum should pass on enduring values, develop pupils' integrity and autonomy and help them to be responsible and caring citizens, capable of contributing to the development of a just society.'

Developing an independent and responsible attitude with children should allow opportunities for spontaneity and enjoyment. Previous experience, professional skill and creative vision shape pedagogy. Additional influences on pedagogy and possible avenues for modification are discussed in Chapter 4. If educational objectives include the development of independence and promotion of opportunities for learning 'how' to learn (Fisher 1996) then the challenge is how to achieve those objectives. Valuing independence requires teachers to know children as learners and to be prepared to find out something of the knowledge, skills and understanding that children bring with them to each situation.

Observation is the most useful tool for determining what children of all ages already know and for monitoring their progress (Blenkin and Kelly 1992; Drummond 1994). Allowing time for observation and interpretation of the evidence may highlight a need for teachers to reconsider personal teaching style and adjust their approach to the curriculum. The chance for genuine communication and discourse will provide further insight into levels of children's understanding. All children need the opportunity to introduce ideas and experiences, to be listened to and to contribute positively to an organic classroom culture.

The cameos at the start of this chapter show young people behaving independently. Children are strongly influenced by cultural experiences that will, in part, be modelled by parents and other adults. In less sophisticated societies children mirror parental behaviour in order to establish the skills needed to contribute to the survival of their group. Do teachers in England see the different independent roles required from children at home as having relevance in school? This will depend on the beliefs, policies and controversies that continue to inform and shape the pedagogy of the teacher (Alexander 2000). Bruner (1996: 47) maintains that 'Teachers have always tried to adjust their teaching to the backgrounds, styles, abilities and interests of the children they teach.' He feels, however, that this does not go far enough and sees more value in bringing children's personal frames of reference 'out of the shadows of tacit knowledge' and helping children to share them with others. This approach gives teachers the opportunity to learn more about children's thinking and to help children to 'think about their thinking'.

The context

Views of children's independence have ranged along a continuum from the perceived 'laissez-faire' attitude of the 1960s, where children were supposed to have made unchecked choices and adults were allegedly discouraged from intervention, to the idea that an independent learner works alone at tasks allocated by adults. If we believe that a positive attitude to learning and an under-standing of emotional security are key factors for children's development, then these two extreme views of independence are both flawed. The child left to 'discover', without adult stimulation, will generally fail to move beyond Vygotsky's Zone of Actual Development. The child working in isolation without help will reinforce misconceptions and become conditioned to repress the desire to inquire and to put forward hypotheses. The *interactionist* view of independence, suggested from the survey teachers' re-sponses, provides a balance between these two approaches. This view sits at midway on the *independence continuum*. It acknow-ledges the need that children have to explore freely and to communicate as necessary. It also recognizes that working alone will be appropriate when the time is right.

Classrooms are the contexts in which formal education takes place. They reflect both the political and cultural effects of con-stantly changing educational perspectives. An independent approach to learning may be seen as unrealistic for children taught in classes of thirty. The prescribed curriculum and the chain of targets, tests and expectations increase teachers' doubts about providing an independent approach to teaching and learning. Merry (1998) writes of increasing internal and external contem-porary pressures that preclude independence. Teachers, however, need to understand what children are thinking; what they are thinking about thinking and where their thinking is coming from. This will influence how the most can be made of the curriculum offered to children. Teachers need to embrace this consciousness or meta-cognition and relate it to a climate of specific curriculum accountability and narrow assessment pressures.

The culture of the school and the culture of the home

Pollard (1996) suggests that the classroom should reflect the cultural background of children. The cultural background of any group of children will be characterized by its diversity. Class-room practice will be the result of realistic decisions and pragmatic compromises. From a practical standpoint the classroom cannot reflect the experiences of all children, but it should allow children to build on their existing cultural expertise. Encouraging children to share their experiences in daily dialogue and individual and

group interactions can contribute to a mutually adapted intellectual and practical curriculum experience. There are, however,
cautionary questions.

- Which children's experiences will be most important in this
  daily dialogue?
- Will *all* children's contributions be acceptable for the development of curriculum experience?

In Cameo 2 the children show a lack of motivation. They are
capable of solving the problem, but are not interested in its
outcome. As they work, Darren reveals something of his home
experience. He belongs to a secure social group where he has

Figure 1.1   Children will have different responsibilities – Flora and
Fanny with 6-month-old Joseph in Malawi, Central Africa

learned related attitudes and skills. He is able to discuss his interest, expectations and motivation. In Cameo 3 the children have social responsibilities that take account of their age and their sex. The survival of their group depends on the specific contribution of its members. These children have to be independent from an early age. Their independence is related to the interdependence of the family and the wider group members. Their limited education and poor nutrition will stand in the way of many of them developing a vision for educational and financial independence. They have responsibilities to their group that preclude a chance for independent thought and autonomy.

Children in England are a part of various social groups. As group members they have specific expectations placed upon them and are exposed to a variety of attitudes. Do teachers acknowledge children's personal experiences and recognize them as an integral part of individual development and as a source of contributions to the curriculum?

The reality of classrooms

Classrooms provide a contrived learning environment for children, with tasks, equipment and social interactions found only in schools (Holt 1965; Donaldson 1978; Tizard and Hughes 1984; Merry 1998; Whitebread 2000). These environments often place constraints on provision for an independent approach to teaching and learning. Allowing children to be independent requires acknowledgement of children's potential for responsibility and recognition that varying levels of independence will be realized when children are trusted to respond in relevant but sometimes challenging ways. In this way *self-image* and *self-esteem* will develop (Merry 1998). Building self-image must take place in an environment where the response to children's skills and knowledge is positive and where their diverse experiences are celebrated. Homes do not offer the same range of resources, carefully planned activities or concentration on curriculum outcomes that are available in schools. The strength of learning at home, however, lies in the provision of opportunities for solving everyday problems, where there is knowledge of children's prior experience and adults are often quick to offer support.

Encouraging an independent attitude in classrooms

Many of the survey teachers see the need to provide:

- an ethos that encourages confidence and shared management that is understood by adults as well as children;
- an opportunity for children to contribute to classroom organization and management;
- open-ended, relevant projects, materials, tools and strategies that help children to persevere and think for themselves;
- an opportunity for children to take time over projects, with allowance for recording and assessing their learning;
- a secure, calm atmosphere that encourages motivation;
- personal space for children to work and to store belongings and precious objects.

The survey teachers also see good communication as essential for developing independent classrooms. Children's views are valued and time is made available for sharing knowledge, discussing, reviewing, reporting, predicting and questioning. Collaborative talk is considered to be important, especially where there is time for story telling, role-play and imaginative play.

What governs life in classrooms?

The rules and procedures in the classroom affect the experiences of those who work in them (Cook and Finlayson 1999). The teachers see the interpretation of rules and procedures that result from legislation and initiatives putting pressure on an independent attitude to learning. Some of the influences on pedagogy and classroom organization and management are investigated in Chapter 4. The 'progressive' movement of the 1960s, with its child-centred ideal, is an example of a powerful influence that has faded but never died. Alexander (2000: 532) describes the current English education system as 'centralized' and 'over policed', but recognizes a 'professional consciousness' that allows for definite continuity in 'progressive idealism' in spite of 'modernization'. Merry (1998: 57) says that 'in Western society, at least, an all-pervading aim of child-centred education has always been to encourage children to learn for themselves'. This, in part, offers hope for teachers, who feel that their classrooms must reflect the reality of children's development and the desire they have to achieve an independent approach to teaching and learning.

Planning for learning

The survey teachers provided a variety of views on planning. It was seen by some to be important for children to have some responsibility for their planning. The High/Scope approach was referred to. They looked at the value of children making their own plans and reviewing the outcomes after work (Chapter 5). Teachers of older children were clear that allowing children to be involved in planning was important but they found it harder to allow the necessary time and space. Discussion indicated that teachers felt they should:

- allow children to plan some of their activities and give them opportunities for negotiation in the order of tasks for the week;
- give children use of a 'planning board' on which to organize their tasks;
- remember that children need to have the opportunity to work at personal tasks;
- encourage the development of personal action plans;
- use posters and flow charts to remind children how to solve particular problems;
- ensure that all tasks in the classroom give opportunities for children to contribute ideas, exercise independence and maintain at least some cultural identity.

The teachers generally valued children's ideas on organization, management and maintenance. They saw easy access to appropriate materials as making an important contribution to independence, as well as time spent discussing health and safety issues. Some teachers welcomed children's views and contributions when the structure and pattern of classrooms was being reviewed. For discussion of effective classroom organization consult Moyles 1992, 1995; Fisher 1996.

The child

Varying degrees of independence will be a part of all children's lives and it is the responsibility of schools to recognize that continuity of opportunities for independence will benefit children and adults. Provision for independence in classrooms requires children to have a voice and to contribute positively to the climate of the classroom. Children are being educated in order that they will contribute to the economy, democracy and social justice of society (Alexander 1995). They are also being educated to achieve their potential, in a climate of changing perspectives of childhood, education and society. The skills and knowledge that children are developing beyond the school environment should complement the school curriculum. Listening to children and respecting their experiences will help them to develop their intrinsic motivation, enhance their self-esteem and allow them to feel valued as members of the learning community.

A view of education that advocates an independent approach to teaching and learning can present problems. It may be labelled as 'progressive', 'radical', 'child-centred' or simply unrealistic. While acknowledging that views will vary, it is important not to accept ideas that suggest that children have short concentration spans, limited capabilities and an inability to think for themselves. Discussions with some of the survey teachers revealed a view that motivation can only be maintained through extrinsic rewards, with no importance placed on responsibility and independent operation. The same discussions, however, led to an assertion that a climate of classroom independence is a climate where teaching and learning can go beyond a statutory curriculum: 'The school curriculum . . . should build on pupils' strengths, interests and experiences and develop their confidence in their capacity to learn and work independently and collaboratively' (DfEE/QCA 1999: 11).

Experience of independence in the wider environment

Children who arrive at school with experience of books and stories are assumed to be children who will make significant achievement in literacy (Tizard and Hughes 1984; Wells 1986; Whitehead 1997). How then is the child received who has knowledge of stripping the engine of a car, or the child who poaches pheasants with his father at the weekends? Is there an immediate division in expectation for children whose experiences 'fit' easily into the educational mould and children whose experiences receive negative or indifferent responses? Which group receives encouragement to contribute to the daily dialogue? Merry (1998: 102) talks of the likelihood of a better start for the child 'whose underlying expectations about behaviour at home matches expectations for school behaviour'. Suschitzky and Chapman (1998) agree that the background of the children will have different influences on their levels of independence and on their social skills.

Where cultural expectations fit easily into the 'classroom pattern' will independence be achieved easily, with a rise in self-esteem as an inevitable consequence? It is less easy to understand and accommodate the child whose experience includes dealing with scrap material and who is able to discriminate between ferrous and non-ferrous metal, but is unable to read. Such children are often those who are identified early on as having a deficit and a need for intervention strategies. These are also the children who are less likely to be given opportunities to be independent.

The problem lies not only with children whose cultural experiences are outside the 'school culture', but with the lack of recognition of the prior experience of *all* children. Views expressed by the Scottish Consultative Council on the Curriculum (Caddell 1998) consider that the mismatch in mathematics, for instance, starts from the early years. It is suggested that children who have had relevant number knowledge from their homes frequently fail to make any links with their early number experience in school. This is reiterated in Hughes (1986); Thompson (1997); Atkinson (1992) and Montague-Smith (1997). The contrast is made between the mathematical problems that occur naturally and spontaneously in the home and those that are contrived and timetabled in school. Knowledge of children's prior, culturally determined experiences is only one aspect of structuring an appropriate curriculum for all children. It is, however, an aspect that should be more fully considered if we are to provide a mutually beneficial, independent curriculum approach. The National Advisory Committee on Creative and Cultural Education (1999) says that the ways of life or the cultures of groups are often very complex. Recognition that these influences exist must surely benefit independent and creative experiences for all children.

Finding out what children know

Baseline assessment for children provides numerical scores for their attainment during the first seven weeks in a reception class (until 2002; the assessment is about to be moved to the end of the reception year) (Lindsay and Desforges 1998). Children are assessed against a standard checklist (Sainsbury 1998). This procedure takes little account of the wider range of skills and attitudes that children have developed or are developing in the home situation. Skills and attitudes depend on the contextual and cultural requirements of the child's home environment. As the education experience unfolds, so the school 'checklists' and summative assessments increase and children are rapidly led down a curriculum route that may not motivate them or encourage them to be independent. When targets for their learning are predetermined from an early age it may be hard for children to make creative responses to problems and provide intelligent reflection on outcomes. Cameos 2 and 3 illustrate examples of responsibility offered to children outside the school environment and the importance of the home as an environment for learning. Children's prior knowledge, skills and understanding should be relevant to the pattern of education. How to encourage and sustain an independent attitude is, however, a puzzle for some teachers.

In the handbook on the National Curriculum for primary teachers (DfEE/QCA 1999: 11) it is stated that the curriculum should . . . 'build on pupil's strengths, interests and experiences and develop their confidence in their capacity to learn and work independently and collaboratively'. The curriculum guidance for the foundation stage (DfEE/QCA 2000: 12) also suggests that 'the learning environment should provide a structure for teaching within which children, explore, experiment, plan and make decisions for themselves . . .'

What is the impact on the learner of being independent?

The survey teachers saw independent children as developing skills that help them to further their own learning by:

- using their own ideas to form opinions and having the confidence to test them out;
- solving problems, taking risks and using a range of strategies to deal with situations;
- tackling problems relevant to their own experience and relating them to situations led by the teacher;

- taking responsibility and understanding the consequences of their actions;
- understanding that physical and social boundaries have to be observed;
- developing analytical, reflective and systematic thinking skills.

Reassuringly, there is evidence from the survey group of recognition of children's prior knowledge, with independent children seen as able to 'tackle problems relevant to their own experience'. Could Darren (Cameo 2) be given problems related to his knowledge of the internal combustion engine, in order to complement and extend his specific technical skills and understanding? The survey showed that risk taking, problem solving, responsibility for personal actions, reflection and revelation were all seen, by some teachers, to be key attributes for children's learning. Chapter 6 offers an excellent illustration of children using all these strategies to work together harmoniously, while exercising independence and individuality.

Independent children have a sense of well-being

The survey teachers feel that independent children show:

- self-motivation and self-esteem and an increase in their social and physical confidence;
- less need to seek attention;
- reluctance simply to follow peers, because they are able to make their own decisions with less worry about being wrong;
- a healthy respect for their peers and for the environment;
- the ability to take responsibility in group situations;
- constructive time management and self-discipline;
- qualities that ensure trust and respect from adults;
- active and energetic rather than passive learning;
- satisfaction from personal and collective triumphs;
- the ability to communicate and to express feelings;
- confidence and opportunity to take risks and to work to a personal agenda;
- enjoyment of challenges.

Well-being and involvement have been the subject of research and are useful concepts for practitioners who want to improve the quality of their interaction with children. Many claims for the importance of well-being have been carefully observed and sensitively recorded by Laevers (1997, 2000). He identifies particular signals shown by children who have a sense of well-being. These include openness, flexibility, self-confidence and self-esteem, vitality, relaxation and inner peace (Arnold 2001). However, will *all* children be given the chance to experience these attributes? Chapter 5 provides a view of equality of opportunity and an independent approach to teaching where an inclusive ethos and positive behaviour management ensure that everybody has an opportunity to contribute to the culture of the classroom.

Independent children work to a higher standard

Further discussion with the survey teachers provides a view that independent children work to a higher standard. They are seen as able to:

- become thoroughly involved with their work, with more chance that tasks will be completed successfully;
- seek information from a range of sources and set personal expectations for achievement;
- demonstrate a positive attitude to learning, take pride in work, show initiative and evaluate outcomes;
- recognize their own skills and be realistic about what they know and what they do not understand;
- move confidently in their own space and try to meet personal needs;
- work collaboratively and seek information and assurance from peers and adults;
- see relevance in the curriculum and have ownership of aspects of learning;
- show concern for peers and offer help when necessary.

Children were observed to be working independently and to a very high standard in the Reggio Emilia schools in northern Italy (Knight 2001). (Chapter 5 provides an overview of the Reggio Emilia approach to teaching and learning.) It is very significant, however, to find that the survey teachers also observed high standards of work when children's independence was valued.

The next theme that came out of the survey considers the noticeable social adeptness of independent children.

Independent children are more socially adept

The survey teachers' views on the social impact of independent children is that they are:

- more socially aware;
- able to offer support for peers;
- part of a group that does not always need to be told what to do;
- able to find a place in a social group where they can contribute with confidence.

Is this social confidence something that any child will be able to achieve? There is still an indication that the chance for independence is not offered to *all* children.

Many teachers talked about the pressures on them to satisfy curricular demands and prescribed targets. They talked of time restraints and lack of personal confidence. They talked also of peer pressure and pressure from head teachers that caused them to keep children at low-level tasks as long as they assumed a 'working pose'! A few were conscious that sharing their real feelings about independence might seem spurious if they reflected on what really happened in their classrooms. These teachers were guilty about the mismatch between their desire for an independent ethos and their concern for the demands of the curriculum. They were concerned that they needed strategies to help them to realize their belief in an independent approach to teaching and learning.

Social and emotional considerations

Some of the teachers discussed the social and emotional benefits gained by independent children. They saw children:

- developing confidence when responsive adults support and extend their ideas;

- being encouraged to develop individuality and given praise and support that helps to develop self-worth;
- being listened to even when their ideas and responses are not what the teachers had expected;
- having a sense of mutual trust with teachers and a feeling of ownership of aspects of learning;
- having pride in a shared environment;
- having personal feelings and difficult situations resolved through individual discussions or whole-class meetings;
- being encouraged to work with others to help solve problems and to share in the school community.

As the century unfolds the introduction of initiatives will undoubtedly continue. The current literacy and numeracy strategies are not explored in detail in this book. It is interesting to reflect, however, that 'independent work' in the National Literacy Strategy (DfEE 1998: 12) requires that 'pupils should be trained not to interrupt the teacher and there should be sufficient resources for them to fall back on if they get stuck'. This interpretation of independence will influence the pedagogy of this generation of teachers. How this restrictive code for independence equates with the survey teachers' broader aims for independence is explored in Chapter 5.

Conclusion

Discussion with teachers has revealed fairly positive views of 'independent' classrooms. Independence has been shown to have two distinct interpretations. The first has been termed the 'isolationist' view where children are required to work alone without recourse to adults. The second is termed the 'interactionist' view, where children have the confidence to investigate, research and seek help as appropriate. It seems that a balance has to be struck between these approaches, to maintain efficient curriculum organization as well as organization for intellectually creative responses. However, little reference was made to the skills, knowledge and understanding that children bring to school with them. Is there an assumption that this prior knowledge will be automatically replaced with experience in school? Is there also an assumption that when children start their formal education they start from square one, put their prior knowledge and experience behind them, and become trained to comply and conform? Are expectations for children in schools inadvertently concerned with a deficit model of childhood? Bruner, cited in Holt (1965: 165), suggests that children in school may well be 'led to believe they don't know or can't do something they knew, or could do, before they got to school'. In order to maintain and extend an independent approach to teaching and learning teachers need to maintain confidence in providing appropriate experiences for children in spite of the inevitable constraints. Placing more value on children's prior understanding and encouraging their expertise may well be a powerful way to achieve an independent classroom. Teachers have an exciting challenge to organize and manage classroom environments that encourage the development of independent, caring and responsible citizens.

Questions

1 How much do you know about the responsibilities, skills and understanding that are a part of children's lives outside school?
2 How do you feel about the level of independence in your own classroom?
3 Is it possible for all children in the same class to have the same degree of independence?

2

Communication and independence: 'What did you say in school today?'

Cameo 1

A group of 5-year-old children watch a teacher cutting fruit.

Teacher: (cuts apples) We'll cut out the pips so now we've got 1,2,3 . . .

Jamie: I like the pips in.

Teacher: What will the pips grow into if you plant them in the soil?

Sara: Another apple tree.

Teacher: (nodding) That's right, the pips will grow into an apple tree. The pips in the apples are the seeds. Now try to remember what the red apple tasted like. The apple you had yesterday. (Teacher hands out the apple pieces) When you have a piece of green apple in your mouth see if it tastes the same or a little bit different.

Sara: I ate all my red apple.

(A man arrives carrying half a watermelon. He hands it to the teacher.)

Teacher: Good gracious, I think that we'll need a great big knife to cut this up!

Jamie: It's got pips as well. It's juicy.

Teacher: I think these pips are like pomegranate pips. I think we can eat watermelon pips.

Sara: Do you have to put them in your mouth and then they grow into that big melon?

Teacher: They grow into another watermelon. Watermelons grow in a different country from this country. Shall we think about the apples again?

Isaac: (picks up the melon) It's very heavy to hold!
Teacher: Shall we think about the apples again? (takes the melon from Isaac and asks him to sit down) You liked the apples you've just been eating didn't you? Were they crunchy or were they soft?
Jamie: Soft.
Teacher: Sit down . . . no, you've had yours. Was yours soft?
Nancy: (nods)
Teacher: Now we've got two bananas to cut up!
Sam: (picks up the melon) It's heavier than an elephant!

Cameo 2

Ten 4-year-old children are taking part in a 'review time' (an element of the High/Scope curriculum discussed further in Chapter 5) following the morning activity. Carrie and Mitzie are talking to the group about the results of the work they had planned.

Teacher: . . . Off you go, girls, tell us about your morning.
Carrie: I did a drawing, put it in this envelope and it's in the envelope. I'm not telling you what's in the envelope, you'll have to guess!
Mitzie: Shall I tell you what's in my envelope?
Carrie: Can you guess what's in this wrapping paper?
Mitzie: Guess what's in mine?
Teacher: Can we guess first what's in Carrie's? I can't remember what you said Carrie. What did you say when you did your planning?
Mitzie: I think she said the 'drawing area'.
Teacher: (to the group) What did she say she was going to put on her paper?
Child 1: Spider.
Child 2: Ladybird.
Carrie: No.
Teacher: Can you give us a clue, Carrie?
Carrie: It starts with an 's' sound. It's 's' for zebra.
Teacher: Yes, zebra does sound like an 's'.
Mitzie: Miss Lloyd, why did the animal cross the road?
Carrie: Why did the zebra cross the road? Because there's a zebra cross and it's stripy.

Cameo 3

Two 10-year-old girls, Jade and Emma, are writing an alternative ending to the story of 'Red Riding Hood'. The teacher moves between groups of children at the computers and listens to their conversations.

Jade: I think that we should make the ending very exciting. They mustn't live happily ever after.

Emma: We must punish the wolf.

Jade: I think if I was Red Riding Hood I would kill the wolf as soon as he leapt out of bed.

Emma: She was only a little girl so how could she kill an animal?

Jade: She might use a knife.

Emma: It wouldn't be in her character.

Teacher: Do we sometimes react to situations in ways that are outside our characters?

Jade: I got angry with my mum and called her a witch when she said that I couldn't watch telly.

Emma: She mustn't have a knife but I wonder what we'll think of?

Introduction

In this chapter the link between independence and powerful verbal and written communication is explored. Vygotsky, while recognizing that children did not use language like adults, saw language in a social context as regulating the actions of others and being internalized to become thinking. Norman (1990: 7) sees spoken language as converting knowledge into understanding and helping members of a group to develop new understanding. Listening to children talking as well as responding to their writing allows adults to have an insight into what children know about language and communication and how they think. Because talk is largely ephemeral and hard to regulate it is often undervalued in classrooms. Indifferent or negative responses to children's verbal communication can be demotivating for children. The development of exciting and genuine verbal interaction between adults and children will have a lasting and positive effect. Too often the meaningful and challenging conversations that children have at home are not in evidence at school. Questioning and explaining are also often seriously underdeveloped (Brown and Wragg 1993). Similarly the process of children's early graphic representation may be misunderstood and the outcomes undervalued.

Writing, even in its very early stages, is a means by which children express their individuality and understanding. If too much emphasis is placed on punctuation, spelling and handwriting then essential risk taking by the writer will be lost and communication forfeited. Examples of writing, encouraged through sharing of ideas and skilful dialogue between adults and children, are presented in this chapter. Encouraging young writers and promoting authorship begins when children start to communicate their thoughts and ideas through their drawing and early mark making. Writing starts as a personal expression of ideas and develops in a variety of ways, in different contexts and in different social and cultural groups (Czerniewska 1992). Children need to feel confident when talking and writing and to understand how communication helps them to clarify their ideas, share messages and make sense of new experiences.

The teacher

Some teachers are sensitive to children's prior knowledge of communication and are skilled in scaffolding ideas and providing challenges. These practitioners build genuine relationships with children and help them to form positive relationships with one another. They provide encouragement for children to draw on home experiences. Children may, however, find a marked difference between communication at home and at school. In school they may no longer be required to converse spontaneously. Verbal exchange in a collaborative environment may be restricted. Some children will find a puzzling adult/child role reversal. In school the adult may control talk and children will be no longer required to interact spontaneously (Urquart cited in Whitebread 2000). The work of Wells (1986) and Tizard and Hughes (1984) provided evidence of the low level of communication between adults and young children in some classrooms. There was concentration on the 'here and now' rather than on children's wider experiences. Redressing any balance of control requires adults and children to establish effective communication partnerships. Increased opportunities for children to take the lead in expressing their ideas trigger sympathetic and challenging responses from adults.

In the National Curriculum (DfEE/QCA 1999: 22) the development of 'thinking skills' is described as a means of 'learning how to learn'. These skills are seen as complementing information processing, reasoning, enquiry, creativity and evaluation. 'Thinking skills' have been an integral part of education in the USA for many years (Costello 2000). Authors writing about young children have already stressed the importance of encouraging children to think (Athey 1990; Nutbrown 1994; Whitebread 1996). With the development of the National Curriculum in England and Wales, thinking about subjects has been more prominent than thinking about the process of thinking and its contribution to learning. The skill lies in providing appropriate experiences to inspire children to think as well as understanding what connections children are making as they think.

Try to remember what the red apple tasted like

In Cameo 1 the teacher had planned a pathway for her 'lesson' and finds it hard to follow the spontaneous responses of the children and to adapt the session to accommodate their thinking and understanding. She is anxious to 'teach' about the characteristics of different apples. She does not consider that a more flexible organizational approach would help the children to make better sense of the situation. The watermelon could have been explored spontaneously. The teacher returns to the discussion of apples and introduces the abstract concept of the taste relating to apples sampled on the previous day.

There is, however, another way to consider the interaction. Whereas Piaget saw children of this age as being incapable of abstract thought, Bruner (1968) provided views on representing the world that saw abstract meaning as something that young children could relate to quite early. The children in Cameo 1 are provided with one piece of green and one piece of red apple on consecutive days. These 4-year-old children surely still need immediate experiences? Bruner describes this as the *enactive* stage. The teacher might, quite rightly, have hoped to adopt an *iconic* stance where representation is introduced either through mental images or pictures. However, she asks the children to create a mental image of the taste and texture of an apple that they can no longer see. This is outside the parameters of their current understanding. These children need more *concrete* experiences and more sensitive extension of the ideas that they offer before they will be ready to adopt a more abstract stance.

Through adherence to her original plan the teacher loses the opportunity to discuss 'melon pips growing in the mouth' or perhaps the difference in taste between a slice of melon and a slice of green apple. The introduction of bananas is the final act of confusion. Imagine a plenary session following this 'lesson'.

Teacher: Can you tell me what we have done this morning?
Children: We tasted apples.
– The green apple was sour but I couldn't remember the red apple because that was yesterday.
– Sam said that the watermelon was 'heavier than an elephant'. I wanted to hold it.
– What's a pomegranate?
– You said we needed a sharp knife to cut up the melon but we didn't cut it up.
– I wanted to taste the watermelon.
– Why were you cutting up bananas?

Summary

1 What were the teacher's objectives for the children's learning?
2 Should the teacher have adopted a more sensitive and flexible approach?
3 How could the teacher have made more of the children's verbal responses?
4 How would shared ownership of the conversation have made a difference to the learning experience?
5 What did the children learn?

Verbal interaction is like a game of tennis

Children need help in formulating thoughts and in gaining confidence in putting forward views. Teachers need help in tuning into children's clues about conceptual understanding. They need to recognize the variety of ways in which children express their thoughts and how thoughts can be developed into more complete concepts. Bruner (1996) talks of a pedagogy that requires teachers to help children to move from private to shared frames of reference. This sharing process should allow individual learning to take place and new opportunities to arise through collaboration. The idea of growing melons from pips after putting the pips in one's mouth (Cameo 1) results from an interesting combination of previous knowledge and an incomplete understanding of seeds and growth. The introduction of pomegranate seeds into the discussion of melon seeds causes unnecessary confusion. Enhancing children's understanding should involve:

- listening to children;
- making informed assessments of their intended meaning;
- thinking before responding.

In the anxiety to establish 'pace' we lose opportunities to draw on children's knowledge and to help them communicate in order to understand genuine turn taking. The ball, or in this case the apple, was definitely *out of court*!

In Cameo 2 the children have been encouraged to take turns, at 'review time'. Both Carrie and Mitzie have control over the dialogue and the teacher acts as an umpire and sometimes a coach. The children show their early understanding of the *joke* genre. They are able to engage with their audience in a guessing game and finally, outside the cameo, to resolve the puzzle they present by declaring that there is a birthday present inside the parcel. This successful interaction can be described as *game, set and match*!

In each cameo the teachers have recognized the importance of classroom discussion for developing thinking skills and encouraging communication (Costello 2000). In the first cameo, however, the children are given little chance to think clearly. The language used by the teacher reinforces the *teacher* stereotype. The teacher uses a transmission method of teaching which does not consider the perspective of the learner (Sotto 1994). These young children needed extended experience of both the 'red apple' and 'the green apple'. This should have been followed by tentative recall, drawing on previous knowledge of texture and taste. As it was, the learning objectives were unclear and the learning potential that was provided by the unexpected entry of the watermelon wasted.

All lessons need to be lessons in thinking (Fisher 1990). Reflective enquiry into all aspects of teaching and learning was at one time considered essential for teachers and children. In the light of a conformist approach to the curriculum it has seemingly become less necessary. If, however, we are to increase children's chances of achieving their potential then there needs to be a return to a pedagogy that promotes general thinking and specific challenge.

When helping children to become independent, teachers need to develop a climate where children make secure attachments. Cognition and emotional development are undoubtedly linked (Urquart in Whitebread 2000) and the child with emotional difficulties will be least likely to become involved, make creative links between areas of knowledge or develop an independent approach to thought and action. As Costello (2000) says, developing thinking requires teachers to intervene when children are offering insight into their cognitive processing. All children need adults' intuitive support and sensitive acceptance to allow intellectual and emotional development to proceed smoothly.

The context

The cameos provide a focused view of contexts for communication. In Cameo 1 we see the type of pitfall experienced by all teachers at some time. The lesson has been planned with an agenda to be followed at all costs. The children are intrigued by the entry of the watermelon. There is acknowledgement of the melon and some discussion but the opportunity for developing the children's curiosity is missed. The teacher controls the interaction and confuses the children.

Cameo 2 presents a short extract from a longer conversation. The children are practising presentation skills as they review their morning's work. They recall, evaluate, tease and tell a 'joke'. For a few minutes the children have the attention of an audience and a chance to express their ideas. Their level of engagement is sophisticated because they are given time to put forward ideas with adult encouragement and sensitive interaction. They are only 4 years old but are already moving towards a Key Stage 2 requirement for the National Curriculum where pupils should be able to 'gain and maintain the interest and response of different audiences . . . by humour (and) varying pace. . .' (DfEE/QCA 1999: 50).

Contexts for writing

In Cameo 3 children are writing together using a computer. They are working on an alternative ending to the story of 'Red Riding Hood'. They discuss, draft, delete, redraft collaborate, compromise and eventually arrive at a finished piece. Listening to their ideas reveals their level of thinking and highlights the important reference made to personal experience. The teacher's intervention is timely and supportive.

Children encouraged to write independently and allowed to experiment freely with technical structures will understand the power of written messages. Adults need to be aware that writing is a sophisticated and abstract method of conveying ideas, feelings and creative responses. The environments in which children work should allow them to gain confidence, 'have a go', and understand the messages that can be conveyed through writing. Children should be encouraged to see themselves as writers and to discuss their ideas seriously with peers and adults. They should be given opportunities to reflect on different registers and styles. Whitehead (1997) discusses 'the complexity and the joy in supporting young children's development as speakers, writers and readers'. In the sections that follow there is support for this statement.

A climate for talking and writing

Children's thinking is revealed as they talk, as well as through their actions. Teachers who understand the link between thought and language can scaffold children as they think out loud. The climate for talk should allow children to collaborate and participate. Opportunities should also be made to encourage children to think for themselves and to share their thoughts with others. Children's thinking is based on their prior experience, the wide range of issues they have to think about and the connections that they are able to make with the classroom situation. Teachers who listen are surprised at the logic and creative connections that children make. When children demonstrate reasoned but imperfect understanding of a concept there is opportunity for adults to respond, encourage and challenge. This gives an opportunity for unravelling and extending thinking that will benefit other children as well as the child in question. Similarly, children's writing should be seen as a natural extension of the desire to communicate through talking. The poignancy and power of written language will further reveal children's developing understanding. Calkins (1986: 31) says that 'when children write we are often overwhelmed by what they reveal to us: so many voices, errors, choices, experiments and hopes'.

The context for talking and writing should include:

- an environment where children are encouraged to communicate and where the purposes for talking and writing are discussed;
- adults and children taking a mutual interest in each other's experiences;
- a climate where listening and responding to one another is valued;
- adults and children sharing initiation of conversations within realistic parameters;
- tentative delivery by the teacher that allows a range of views, questions and assertions to be presented by the children;
- questions and explanations to reinforce children's ideas as well as to challenge their thinking;
- silence and significant pauses that give time for reflection and formulation of ideas;
- opportunities for discussing and writing about topics that are relevant to children and that reflect their lives outside school;
- time for children to think, reconsider and rework;
- sensitivity to the verbal and graphic ability of each child;
- sensitivity to the well-being and mood of particular children, the effect of unpredicted events and the time of the day;
- mutual respect between adults and children;
- an *independent* environment that is aesthetically pleasing and where children will want to talk and to write for various audiences and using a variety of genres.

The child

In school, the process through which a child passes to become independent is often a gradual one. Opportunities for independence in the home will inevitably be more varied. Although many teachers recognize elements of self-organization and independent thinking among the children in their care, the emergence of self-motivated, critical thinkers will be the result of a lengthy metamorphosis. The independent people who emerge will have had positive experiences as well as possible setbacks along the way. Clues about individual future levels of confidence and positive engagement will have been observable in children, even if not quantifiable, from a very early age. Fostering and achieving independence requires sensitivity and confidence on the part of the teacher and perseverance on the part of children. For independence to flourish in classrooms there must be opportunities for all children to communicate their differing as well as collective viewpoints.

The curriculum has 'public demands' (Merry 1998: 66) and these present constraints for teaching and learning. The English National Curriculum is statutory and the danger is that it will be interpreted as 'no more, no less' (Alexander 2000: 156). In an anxiety to achieve curriculum objectives it is easy to forget how children develop. A requirement for teachers to have knowledge of child development has, however, returned as a focus for the early years curriculum. Knowledge of continuing development and children's progress is also just as important for teachers of older children.

Approaches to curriculum organization will always vary (Sotto 1994; Alexander 1995) even though statutory recommendations, national initiatives, local trends and intervention programmes abound. With the introduction of the National Curriculum the intention was that, although bodies of knowledge and predetermined goals were to be introduced, the delivery of the curriculum would still be the preserve of the teacher. This intention has, in part, been superseded by alternative directives, concerned with prescriptive delivery, particularly in the area of literacy.

Across the primary curriculum children may be receiving whole-class experience for long periods of time. Whole-class teaching was seen by Alexander *et al.* (1992: 28) to be an essential skill for advancing pupils' thinking through using 'higher order questioning, explanations and questions'. They recognized, however, possible disadvantages for children of receiving insufficient challenge. They saw a tendency for teaching to be pitched at the midpoint of the ability range. Thus there is a danger that an overemphasis on collective teaching will not take into account children's differing needs as communicators, particularly in the early years. Talking has become less important in classrooms. This is a problem if we are to believe that failure to listen to talk 'is to miss out on a vital opportunity to learn about children's thinking' (Hall and Martello 1996: vi). Teachers often fail to recognize children's learning because ideas are not articulated in standard terms. Teachers also need to ensure that the terminology they use is fully understood by the children.

Children communicating with adults

Effective verbal interaction and communication between children and adults has a two-way benefit. Children gain confidence in trying out ideas and experimenting with new vocabulary and structures and teachers, by listening and responding sensitively and appropriately, are able to learn about children's existing knowledge (Tizard and Hughes 1984; Wells 1986) and recognize the emergence of conceptual frameworks (Nutbrown 1994; Whitebread 1996).

In Cameo 2 both Mitzie and Carrie share a joke about zebras and pedestrian crossings. In the short dialogue Mitzie recalls that 'an animal' crosses the road. Carrie on the other hand makes the connection between the pattern on the animal called a zebra and the pattern on the crossing. She does not understand the play on words. Information about the thinking processes used by the two children is apparent from this short interchange. There is also evidence of the verbal interaction that had gone on in Carries's home (Tizard and Hughes 1984). The girls begin to tell jokes, and by listening to them the teacher gains knowledge of the wider language and cultural experience of the children.

Suschitzky and Chapman (1998) write about aspects of language that are put in the cupboard and only used after school. The more use that is made of the language that could come out of the cupboard, the easier it is for a climate of mutual understanding to be achieved. Sharing home life and experience in the wider community, through communicating and listening, influences the conceptual thinking of individuals. Whitehead (1997) says that teachers with knowledge of the language culture of the home as well as knowledge of children's developmental stage will provide a more relevant curriculum.

Learning and appropriate experience

Real learning comes about after appropriate experiences (Sotto 1994). Confident use of language by the learner provides evidence of thinking and understanding. The premise for this chapter is that independent thinking can promote observable understanding through use of language and actions. In each cameo the children are using language to explore ideas. In the first cameo, the transmission mode of teaching, with the teacher maintaining control, results in limited and uncertain participation from the children. The teacher is not listening to the children's interjections and responses. These young children will soon learn that only certain interactions will receive approval and they will respond accordingly (Holt 1965; Sotto 1994). They are learning that the teacher is in control and is looking for predetermined responses.

The children in Cameo 3 are familiar with working in pairs as well as in small groups where they have opportunities for discussion and reflective thinking. In this short extract they draw on their knowledge of 'character' to determine possible reactions to the wolf in 'Red Riding Hood'. The teacher's intervention is timely. She asks, 'Do we not sometimes react to situations that are outside our character?' This triggers reflection on a situation encountered at home. Being able to move between reality and fantasy allows the children the chance to take their ideas forward. These children are demonstrating the ability to internalize previous experience and draw on it to make creative connections with the requirements for their current task. They are operating in Bruner's *symbolic* mode. They draw on experience and use powerful images to shape their story ending. To support their writing they have knowledge of the fairytale genre and of writing for an audience. The ending to their story is included later in the chapter.

Confidence in communication

The 'maturational' or 'readiness' perspective on early communication and literacy stemmed from a Piagetian view of sequential stages of development. Perspectives change and a belief in the 'socio-cultural' dimension of literacy learning gives a clearer picture of the reality of children as communicators. It encompasses their development as competent speakers with their development in reading and writing. Donaldson (1978) presented different perspectives on Piaget's work. She presented children with tasks in meaningful contexts and ensured that they could make sense of them. Children at what Piaget described as the *pre-operational* stage were then found to be capable of rational thought. More recently, Donaldson (1992) discusses a theory of movement from action to internalized language or thought. Merry (1998) describes the first stage of development as the *Point Mode* where thinking is taking place at a point in time. A child from Cameo 2, operating in this mode, might say, 'I like this piece of green apple.' The second stage of operation Merry describes as the *Line Mode*, which might result in a child saying, 'Yesterday I had a piece of red apple, I liked that as well.' A link is being made between the present and the immediate past. The third stage Merry describes as the *Construct Mode* where a child might say, 'I like the green apples but the red apples are nicer for a snack.' At this point the child is constructing personal understanding of his or her preference for red apples. The fourth stage, the *Transcendent Mode*, might be applied to the child able to rationalize why he or she prefers red apples to green apples by saying, 'Red apples are much sweeter and softer than green apples.' Thus concrete interaction with apples has led to the child internalizing thoughts and language and expressing comparative thinking. Children operating along this continuum are making sense of situations by drawing on real experiences and going through clear changes in their ability to access information, internalize it and use it to draw conclusions. The teacher in Cameo 1 does not recognize the parameters within which her children are operating. On the other hand, in Cameo 2 Mitzie and Carrie are encouraged to experiment with language in a familiar group. They have previous knowledge of jokes and are gaining confidence in experimenting with language and talking to an audience.

Independence and writing

Communication through writing needs similar encouragement. Through early representation children establish schema or patterns of repeatable behaviour (Athey 1990). These early observable actions are the result of internalizing actions and events experienced in the environment (Meade and Cubey 1995). Piaget (1959: 357) believed that thought 'consisted of internalised and co-ordinated action schemas'. Studies of early writing as well as theoretical and practical discussion of communication through writing are well documented (Kress 1982; Calkins 1986; Temple *et al.* 1988; Hall 1989; Czerniewska 1992; Whitehead 1997). It is important to note that the examples of writing included in this chapter result from learning situations where early graphic representation and emergent writing have been valued and children have been given some ownership of the writing process.

In Cameo 3, Jade and Emma are confident writers. Their previous experience has influenced their thinking and helped to develop a sense of audience and an appropriately defined register for their writing. The children were committed to the process and understood the purpose of conveying written messages. The National Curriculum places emphasis on the structure and purpose of children's writing. This includes being able 'to imagine and explore feelings and ideas, focusing on creative uses of language and how to interest the reader' (DfEE/QCA 1999: 57). The examples of writing that follow are taken from a range of contexts but all the 'writers' show an independent approach to communication.

A new ending for the story of 'Red Riding Hood' by Jade and Emma

The girls (Cameo 3) spend 40 minutes working on their story ending. After discussing a range of gruesome conclusions they decide that the wolf needed punishment but also a chance to repent.

Red Riding Hood was so happy to have her granny back. She knew that the wolf must be punished. She asked the hunters to go hunting and catch the wolf. They brought him back and she told him off. 'You know that what you did is wicked don't you? Now you are going to live in a zoo for two years but first of all you have to say sorry to my granny.'

The wolf looked a bit surprised but he went to Red Riding Hood's granny and said, 'I am very ashamed.' Granny smiled. Red Riding Hood said, 'Now it's time to go to the zoo.' The hunters took the wolf in their big van and children went to the zoo to see <u>The Animal that Wanted to Eat a Granny</u>. The wolf was let out after two years and led a better life.

(Jade and Emma, aged 10)

The children have an understanding of moral issues and issues of fairness. The initial, sensitive intervention from the teacher has encouraged them to develop their thoughts and complete the task efficiently and independently.

Sophie sends a message (5 years)

Sophie is 5 years old. From an early age she sent short, hand-written messages to say 'thank you' and to convey snippets of information to close friends. She found handwriting tedious and this restricted the content of her communications. When using email she became more independent and was able to send detailed and thoughtful messages.

Sophie's message has been written with a pencil but at what cost? She found pencil control hard, although she had a clear idea of the composition of her messages. She was very young to be required to cope with transcription even though she had an understanding of the abstract relationship between the words and their meaning. Word processing proved to be a means of communication that enabled Sophie to send more detailed messages.

Figure 2.1 'To Jill I have made a necklace From love Sophie-Millie and mummy'
At 5 years of age Sophie found pencil control very hard

Sophie emails a message after a friend offered to 'babysit'.

---

04 March 2000

to jillthacyiu freo ofreing that was very cid fero you to oferiwd love you tolove fromsohie m

To Jill,
Thank you for offering. That was very kind for you to offer. I would love you to. Love from Sophie M

Jill's reply

---

06 March 2000

Sophie this is such fun! We can talk often on email now. I am looking forward to seeing you both and I will read to you while mummy and daddy are at your school. Will Millie be a good girl?

Sophie's reply

---

06 March 2000

tojillmillie mit be good or bad or helpful or cind or norty.i will tel you houw to chaj millies napy if you don't know houw to do it.it is owkayif you no houw tolove fromsophie m

To Jill,
Millie might be good or bad or helpful or kind or naughty. I will tell you how to change Millie's nappy if you don't know how to do it.
It is OK if you know how to. Love from Sophie M

Holly (6 years)

Holly wrote at home and in school. She developed an early understanding of the writing process and the range of communication possible when using different genres. The support

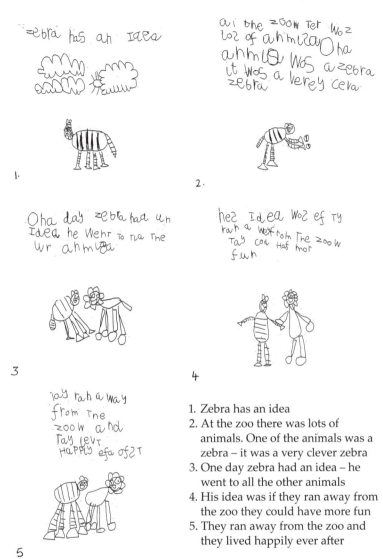

zebra haS ah Idea

1.

ai the zoow Tet woz loz of ahmuzay ha ahmu was a zebra zebra a verey ceva.

2.

.Oha day zebra had uh Idea he wehr to rua The wr ahmua

3

hez Idea woz ef Ty rah a wey from The zoow Tay coa Has mor fuh

4

iay rah a way from Tne zoow and Tay levt Happiy efa of2T

5

1. Zebra has an idea
2. At the zoo there was lots of animals. One of the animals was a zebra – it was a very clever zebra
3. One day zebra had an idea – he went to all the other animals
4. His idea was if they ran away from the zoo they could have more fun
5. They ran away from the zoo and they lived happily ever after

Figure 2.2   Zebra has an idea

for communication in her school was imaginative. There was understanding of the development and interests of individual children. At 6 years of age Holly wrote reference books and story books. Her motivation and enthusiasm for writing was shown in school and at home. *Zebra Has an Idea* is an example of a story written and illustrated by Holly when she was at home. The simplicity yet directness of her plot and the sophistication and gentle humour of her illustrations show her independence as a writer and communicator.

Daniel (11 years)

This child had experienced a very sensitive approach to writing. In his early writing he had experimented and taken risks. He had learned essential transcription skills and had read and critically analysed a range of literature. As a terminally sick child he had had many periods in hospital. The power in the following piece lies in his detailed recollection of sound, smell, sight and touch. Daniel brings together these images into a simple but effective cameo that describes universal experiences of children in hospital. The story is told from the patient's viewpoint but he is able to empathize with others and is aware of an audience. Ernest Hemingway, his favourite author at the time, influenced his writing. Daniel finds an independent and creative outlet for his thoughts. His writing is confident and the climate for writing, in which he had thrived, encouraged children to find a voice and develop strategies for successful authorship.

Parallel Lines

Parallel lines of light appeared on the various dull surfaces that neighboured the window. A grimy venetian blind hung in front of the window, its slats half open. The boy stirred in a distressed manner. He grasped the creased sheets and lay still. He waited. The ward was waking. Nurses clinked up and down between tasks. Urine bottles clattered and babies bawled. A stench of disinfectant circulated the ward. A typical hospital smell. It clung to your clothes. Glass cubicles secluded some patients from the ward. Their pinched, pathetic faces became engraved on the giant panes of glass. They longed to roam free on the brown tiled corridor.

The boy, now fairly familiar with his surroundings, knelt up on the monstrous bed. He had been visited by a generous nurse (that is in size) who clutched a small thermometer in her podgy hand. The boy hunched his puny shoulders. The nurse thrust the thermometer under his arm and said, 'hold it there for three minutes'. The daunting word, 'doctor' was mentioned. They filed in one by one each holding peculiar instruments. Each studied the clipboard at the end of the bed, headed *Patient's Progress*. When they had each had a good prod and poke, they filed out.

After the boy had exchanged a few hand signals with the fellow in the neighbouring cubicle, he settled down to an afternoon nap only to be disturbed by metallic footsteps ringing down the corridor. There was the familiar whine from his brother. The door crawled open. Two beady eyes peered round the bed. A grubby hand lobbed a half-eaten chocolate bar onto the clean sheets. The boy managed to squeeze a smile.

(Daniel, aged 11)

Conclusion

The power of children's communication can be underestimated. The chapter has illustrated aspects of communication and effective ways of helping children to gain a voice. In promoting independence and critical thinking teachers and children must be aware of a variety of opportunities for broadening the curriculum. Chapters 5 and 6 develop this theme further. Cook and Finlayson (1998: 71) describe the environment for learning as 'the climate of the classroom' and it is in a supportive climate that children can show how they are developing through their talk and their actions. As well as respect, sensitivity and the opportunity for problem solving, children need to develop sophisticated levels of communication. They need opportunity to express their views and demonstrate their developing understanding of the world.

Questions about communication

1 How can teachers ensure that children are given a fair hearing in a busy classroom?
2 What classroom changes could you make that would encourage children to talk and write more confidently?
3 Would time be well spent in observing and monitoring communication, and how could children help with this?

3

Motivation and ownership: 'When can I finish my bear?'

Cameo 1

Millie is 14 months old. Using tiny pincer movements with her forefinger and thumb she is picking up spilt red lentils and placing them on a shelf. Karen, her mother, finds Millie a small jar and she continues to pick up the lentils and put them into the container. Millie fetches her doll, and feeds her with the lentils. When 'baby' has had enough Millie smiles and walks away. Karen calls after her, 'I'm going to sweep up the rest of the lentils, Millie. Is that OK?'

Cameo 2

Ten children are sorting a large collection of toy bears and discussing what gives each bear its characteristics. They have been asked to design and make their own bear. The task is supported with an interesting collection of fabrics and other resources. Alice (aged 6) comments, 'I think designing is drawing but we should write things down because a designer needs to remember. I shall use stuffing that is soft so that I can cuddle my bear.' Tom (aged 6) says, 'My bear will walk because he will have separate legs. I want to stuff him with little stones so that he can sit up. I've got some gravel stones on my drive. It must be a strong bear.' Kerry (aged 7) designs her bear quickly, selects her fabric, finds a needle and thread, sets herself apart and completes the task in two hours.

Cameo 3

A group of 9-year-old children is working on a similar 'bear-design' task. They are evaluating the bear collection but are taking longer to start than the previous group. They seem uncertain about what is expected of them and are surprised that they have not been given a pattern to follow. They work painstakingly on their designs but keep asking if they are 'doing it right'. Aaron comments, 'What's the difference between designing and drawing?' Vicky sits for several minutes looking worried and then asks for help. 'I've drawn the head and the body and I've run out of space.' Tim says, 'I can't think how to design and I can't sew.'

Introduction

Motivation and the relationship between motivation and independence are considered in this chapter. Children are intrinsically motivated (Katz and Chard 1990; McNamara 1994). They start to make sense of the world when they are in the womb and from birth onwards caring adults encourage and celebrate their developing independence (Vernon 1971; Sotto 1994). Young babies command the attention of adults, evoking responses and responding in turn (Trevarthen 2000). Any one at any age who has encountered a near death situation will understand that motivation to live is far stronger than can be imagined. Sotto (1994) maintains that motivating someone else requires a particular ability to stimulate and inspire and he sees many teachers as lacking such qualities. Fortunately this is not always true. There are many inspirational teachers who are confident, able to adapt the curriculum requirements to suit their children and who avoid demotivating or disaffecting children (Barrett 1989). On the other hand a transmission style of teaching, where little involvement in practical activity is required, may well demotivate learners. Being motivated is a part of being active and ensures that there is enthusiasm for learning. Teachers should not assume that because they are *teaching* children are necessarily *learning*.

The child

Motivated children have an astonishing ability to work independently. As a young teacher in an inner city school I soon realized that I had much to learn from children whose diverse ethnic backgrounds, preferences and skills were so different from my own. Their motivation and complex problem-solving experience started in home environments where they were learning the Koran, being initiated into the Sikh community, attending African-Caribbean Saturday schools or searching for saleable goods in skips or dumps. Although these children were exposed to important influences outside the culture of the school, they were able to pool their ideas and knowledge and share responsibility for a vibrant and happy atmosphere. They sought new intellectual challenges and made full contributions from their cultural traditions. Parental partnership became very strong and allowed expertise from diverse cultures to permeate the curriculum and the social life of the school.

Motivation will have as much to do with prior experience as to the level of stimulation in the classroom. Chaplain says that individual differences in motivation are not easy to explain. Drawing on attribution theory, he describes three distinct positions which children may adopt. The first is *mastery orientation* where pupils are concerned with achieving personal success for the purpose of learning. The second he describes as *learned helplessness*, which results in children failing to be convinced that they have the ability to succeed, and the third, *self-worth motive* where pupils believe that having the ability is more important than making an effort, and as a consequence they rarely succeed. Without motivation, learning becomes impoverished, but to maintain motivation the climate has to be one in which independence is encouraged and teachers are sensitive to the experiences and knowledge that all children bring to school. Children's intrinsic motivation, or desire to be active learners, is more likely to flourish in classrooms where conditions inspire children and where creativity and imagination are valued (Duffy 1998).

Children feel valued in classrooms where teachers and children understand the expectations that they have of one another. The cameos illustrate opportunities for independent decision making and problem solving. The children are quick to sense the expectations that adults have for their achievements. The children show marked differences in their abilities to solve problems, use creative strategies and complete tasks. 'Teachers are in a position to encourage imaginative and creative thinking or to extinguish it for ever' (Whitebread 2000: 141).

Cameo 1 is based in the home. It provides an example of respect for a young, motivated child and the opportunity given for exploration, even where the activity is seemingly trivial. Children given space and time to work in this way will develop perseverance, more rigorous attention to detail and a more creative approach to learning. These attributes may well provide the key to individual attainment in the future. Millie (Cameo 1) has scope for practising her current behaviour pattern, or schema, which is placing things into containers or holes (Athey 1990; Nutbrown 1999). The dramatic play with 'baby' allows her to represent food with the lentils and to 'post' them into the doll's mouth. The mixture of trust and watchfulness exhibited by Millie's mother, the availability of relevant household materials and the opportunity for spontaneous interaction are all excellent scaffolding for problem solving and learning. Millie is learning through a social constructivist approach, based primarily on '. . . the idea that children actively construct meaning by taking in information and relating it to what they already know . . .' (Merry 1998: 94). Merry goes on to say that children do not learn in isolation but need to express emotions, present attitudes and interact with other people to make the learning effective. Kellmer-Pringle (1992: 33) says that the term social constructivism 'involves the indivisibility of the emotional, cognitive and affective aspects of development' and recognizes willingness or motivation to learn and to make progress.

In Cameo 2 all the children engage immediately with the challenge. Their discussions show that the design task has stimulated their imagination and allowed them to make immediate sense of the requirements for the task. They are able to apply aspects of their previous experience. The teacher has developed a cooperative structure for the classroom that encourages individual as well as group problem solving.

In Cameo 3 the children are reluctant to get started and concerned about the lack of direction for the task. They are used to a didactic style of teaching where progress towards predetermined outcomes is planned for them and where they are concerned to receive adult approval for their finished work.

Cameos 2 and 3 are developed as case studies later in the chapter.

The teacher

Teachers have an enormous responsibility for delivering the curriculum and ensuring that children learn. It is the weight of this responsibility that often constrains them from allowing children to be independent and to have ownership of their work. Galton (1989) considers the frustration in searching for the key that releases creative energy in pupils and teachers.

The Plowden Report (CACE 1967) set the child at the heart of the educational process. The influence of this report was strong and, in spite of much criticism, many of its ideals are still a part of much early years classroom practice. McNamara (1994), however, refutes the child-centred approach and places teachers at the heart of the process. While understanding that teachers need to care for children and to be sensitive to their needs, he sees them as having a mandate to pass on knowledge skills and understanding. Teachers should take every opportunity to ensure that all children's life chances are improved. The seeming dichotomy between these views raises the issue of balance. It also raises questions about the value placed on the learning process as well as on the outcome. McNamara acknowledges that not all children are willing learners and that their unwillingness may be linked to a lack of motivation. He says that learning has, in part, to do with 'the independent achievement of the child'. Children must be 'implicated in' and 'responsible for' their own learning. He presents a gloomy picture of children who will never learn unless they want to and are unwilling to make 'independent' contributions. He sees the teachers' pedagogy as having the most influence on the quality and nature of children's learning. This pedagogy he defines as 'vernacular' and describes it as including adaptation of practice to acknowledge classroom constraints. *Teaching* should be placed at the forefront of the teacher's duty. Ordinary language, based on knowledge of children's backgrounds, personal values and commitment, should be used to communicate knowledge. Perceived curriculum constraints might make such a view seem very attractive. It takes no account, however, of the reality that education should be promoting the multidimensional nature of human development, where social and moral progress is considered just as important as intellectual development.

Children are a part of a human community and it is their emotional, social and moral responsibility that should be being promoted through their education as well as their cognitive development (Blenkin and Kelly 2000). Blenkin and Kelly cite Gardner (1993) for his work on multiple intelligences. To this can be added Edwards *et al.* (1998), who write of the work of Loris Malaguzzi, the pioneer of the inspirational Reggio Emilia approach to education in northern Italy (see Chapter 5).

Are we throwing the baby out with the bath water?

Reflection on a polarized view of education provides a framework for deciding the position that both children and teachers take in learning situations and particularly the effect that pedagogy or teaching style has on growing children. It allows those involved in education to take a rational view of a position where children and teachers can satisfactorily achieve personal, communal and national goals.

Teachers understand that human development follows a general pattern. They also know that genetic inheritance, the environment, cultural expectations and social interaction are just some of the influences that will accelerate or delay this development. Knowledge of these influences should underpin teachers' pedagogy and approach to the curriculum. This knowledge provides a firm foundation for teaching and learning. If teachers value the strength of this viewpoint then they will be alive and alert to finding the best way of implementing educational initiatives and suggestions for curriculum change without 'throwing the baby out with the bath water'.

The changes that have overtaken education in recent years have caused some teachers to have 'a crisis of confidence' (Galton 1995: 1). Lack of confidence was voiced by many of the survey teachers. The extensive demands of the curriculum can, however, be balanced realistically and philosophically with the developmental needs of the children. Teaching and learning takes place in many situations and under a range of philosophical and pedagogical stances. Learning is even possible when children are frightened of the teacher (McNamara 1994). Most of us would probably agree, however, that teaching in an atmosphere of fear does nothing for self-esteem or enthusiasm for learning, and is unlikely to foster a lasting affection for school.

Views of children's existing knowledge: threat, irrelevance or cause for celebration?

Not all experiences in the home will be viewed positively or seem relevant in the classroom context. Darren, Aaron and Winston, in Chapter 1, had an interest in cars far outweighing their interest in the bridge topic. Either Darren's knowledge had not been judged applicable to the curriculum or he had never thought about revealing it. Children's specific knowledge may present a threat to teachers or may simply be rejected as irrelevant in a tightly packed schedule. Teachers will usually welcome children's knowledge when it is demonstrated by children who appear to be 'academically well-motivated' (Chaplain 2000: 98).

Developing an interest in *all* children's experiences will lead to a more dynamic, extended curriculum and will give children and adults a chance to excel in their chosen area of expertise. Tizard and Hughes (1984) found that teachers of young children relied on reference to everyday events and did not draw upon children's ongoing relationship with the outside world. Suschitzky and Chapman (1998: 28) present a delightful cameo highlighting how children's prior knowledge may make aspects of the pre-scribed curriculum irrelevant to them. They describe Edward, a child who has knowledge of electrical circuits from his daily encounter with fairground lighting. Making electrical circuits in the science class seems to be insulting to him. Edward could have provided first-hand experience of his use of circuits had the teacher understood his background. In the anxiety to cover the requirements of the curriculum, the knowledge that children bring with them should not be ignored. Understanding the contribution that Edward could have made to the lesson would have added a new dimension to the lesson and given him experience of owner-ship, motivation and self-esteem.

The context

Motivation and perseverance will flourish in an environment where teachers, as well as children, see themselves as learners and where there is mutual understanding of aims and objectives. Bruner (1996) suggests that, in order to improve learning, teachers need to have an understanding of the experiences and relationships that give children a predisposition to learn. Attitudinal differences in learning are the result of complex influences including social class, sex, age, cultural influence and children's attitudes to school. Key to these differences will be the level of motivation that children bring to school and the nature of the relationships that they have with adults and peers. Bruner highlights the communal nature of learning where cultural expectation is shared and children's particular knowledge becomes a part of the curriculum. He suggests that the educational context should create opportunities for children to explore and to solve problems, with the knowledge that instruction is available and help is at hand.

The disposition of the learners will determine how a particular body of knowledge can be structured and made manageable. Bruner sees knowledge as constructed through the enactive mode, with practical activities appropriate to the learning intentions, the iconic mode, through graphic representation, and the symbolic mode, where concepts become internalized and relationships are made between the activity, the symbols and the laws. Teaching must also take into account the system in place for reinforcement and reward. The question of extrinsic, immediate reward or intrinsic reward that depends on the achievement of individuals is important to consider.

A learning context where motivation can be maintained

It may be useful to consider organizational priorities that will help to maintain children's motivation and enhance learning. These have been developed from responses provided by the teachers in my survey.

Children should experience:

- security and a sensitive approach to their feelings;
- resources that reflect their interests and promote imaginative responses;
- praise and recognition for progress as well as outcomes;
- a chance to evaluate and to make changes;
- effective time management to pursue ideas and complete tasks;
- responsibility and ownership and the chance to defend a position;
- encouragement of inherent motivation;

- sensitive adult intervention;
- the chance to use personal skills and knowledge and to take the lead when appropriate;
- tasks that reflect and complement prior knowledge and understanding;
- wider experiences and genuine challenges that allow them to take risks;
- pride in personal achievement.

The social nature of the learning

In Cameo 1 Millie at 14 months understands:

- that adults in her environment trust her to explore and allow her time to work through an experience and to arrive at a conclusion;
- that her play is taken seriously and her opinion sought;
- that although there are rules to be observed (not eating lentils) she is able to experiment in an environment where there are opportunities for relevant first-hand investigation.

Millie's activity also illustrates the fine balance that exists between the child's motivation and sensitive adult intervention. Millie's mother is her 'partner' who is willing, in Bruner's terms, to 'scaffold' her schematic play and move the 'game' forward. Provision of the pot for the lentils takes Millie from the 'zone of actual development' to the 'zone of proximal development' (Vygotsky 1978). Millie is able to pick up the lentils and place them on the shelf – 'zone of actual development'. Karen, her mother, gives her a jar enabling Millie to extend her game by feeding 'baby' – 'zone of proximal development'.

Millie and her mother were in a home situation where a 'code of behaviour' has been developed between them and the 'curriculum' determined by:

- opportunity, flexibility, time and respect for one another;
- intuitive response from Karen to the lead that Millie gives;
- resources and opportunities that stimulate investigation and promote learning;
- Millie's ability to retain ownership of her play and bring the game to a successful conclusion.

Designing and making a bear: two case studies

The child

The children taking part in this two-day project were from the two schools presented in Cameos 2 and 3:
School 1 – the children were 4–7 years old.
School 2 – the children were 9 and 10 years old.

The children started the project with a collection of toy bears, resources for stitching, stuffing and embellishing, and a collection of fabrics. Needles, scissors, paper and pens were provided and the children were free to access familiar classroom resources. They were asked to investigate the bear collection and to decide on characteristics that differentiated the bears. Their brief was to design and construct their own bear. The project was limited to six hours over two days and was outside the normal curriculum. After an introduction the children worked independently unless they had an insoluble problem.

Observations of the children's motivation, independence, ownership, knowledge, skills and understanding were recorded and the similarities and differences between the responses from the two groups were used to support the subsequent discussion. The attitude with which children approached the task and the skills, knowledge and understanding that they brought to any problems were noted. There was no direct observation of the class teachers but what was known of their teaching styles has been reflected on when considering the different ways in which the children approached the task.

Characteristics of the children's attitudes from observations in both schools

School 1

Motivation and independence

The children were given a collection of toy bears to investigate. They had time to choose resources before starting to create a bear of their own.

- *Immediate interest:* 'I've got one like this at home.' 'This is like my sister's bear.' 'I like working with bears, they're so friendly;

we use them for maths and things.' 'This is fun, my mum will be surprised by me doing sewing.'

- *Enthusiasm:* in the choice of resources – very clear personal ideas on selection of fabric and embellishments (buckles, buttons, etc.).
- *Independence:* 'I know where there are some better scissors, I'll get them for you.' 'The sharp ones are in Penny's drawer.'
- *Careful selection:* fabrics and resources chosen carefully and stored in wallets.
- *Queries:* about the meaning of *design*.
- A *quick start* made to pattern making and designing.

Personal interest

- 'I'll finish mine first!' 'Mine will take a long time because his cloak is difficult. I will have to take him home.'
- 'Can we choose our material now? I want to start very soon or we'll never be finished.'
- 'Do you like these for a necklace?'
- 'I like your bear, he's so tiny.'

The children were soon absorbed in the task:

- Older children gave occasional help to younger children.
- The bears quickly took on personalities.
- Individual skills, such as threading needles, selecting materials and cutting fabric were noted.
- All the children showed an independent approach to the task and their motivation appeared to stem from 'self-worth motive' (Chaplain 2000: 105). The children quickly established themselves as 'designers' and were happy to complete the task to their own satisfaction.

Ownership

Children identified with their bears and held them up from time to time for adult and peer approval.

- 'Can we take our bears home?'
- 'I shall give my bear to my sister.'
- 'I want my bear to sleep with me.'
- 'I took my bear home last night. My dad laughed and my mum said, you didn't do all that sewing did you?'

The pride in their achievements and their eagerness to take the bears home illustrates elements of a suggested *context for maintaining motivation and encouraging ownership* (see previous section).

Knowledge, skills and understanding

- 'This bear sits down if I hold him. I shall make him a proper sitting bear. I shall put gravel stones in him. We've got some at home. My dad won't mind.'
- 'I can do all the cutting out.'
- 'How do we make the arms and legs separate?'
- 'We've done sewing before but these needles are sharp. My mum showed me how to thread a needle.'
- 'I sew with my gran. My dad sews his buttons on.'
- 'I don't cut right on the line because you need room for the stuffing, don't you?'
- 'You could stuff a bear with grass, but it might smell like silage or if it was dry it would be hay.'
- 'These scissors are beautiful, they cut so well.'

The children's skill with tools and textiles was impressive. Ritchie (1995: 141) talks of the need to teach children 'to mark, cut and join textiles in a variety of ways, before they can make use of these techniques in solving problems'. These children had never used textiles in school, but were able to apply skills and knowledge learned in other situations. They demonstrated *mastery orientation* with their determination to succeed at all costs (Chaplain 2000).

Evaluation of a bear design: Tom, aged 7 years

> *Observer:* Has your bear worked out the way you thought?
> *Tom:* It's all right but it doesn't sit up by itself.
> *Observer:* Do you know why that is?
> *Tom:* I thought it would be like a 'Beanie', if I put gravel in it.
> *Observer:* Do you know why it didn't work out like a 'Beanie'?
> *Tom:* No, but I'll have look at my sister's 'Beanies'.

During the second week Tom brought a 'Beanie Bear' (a popular toy at the time) from home. He compared it with his gravel-filled bear. 'I know', he said. 'The Beanie Bear is all sort of in one piece.

Figure 3.1 'I shall make him a proper sitting bear. I shall put gravel stones in him.'
Tom, aged 7 years

My bear has got a head and arms and things and they sort of flop.' The observer commented, 'Perhaps you could write to the Ty [manufacturers of Beanies] company?' to ask how their bears are constructed and why they are self supporting.

School 2

The second group of children was also given a collection of toy bears to investigate. They had time to choose resources before starting to create a bear of their own. The children were keen to start but very apprehensive about how to tackle the open-ended task. They needed support, adult approval and encouragement to continue. The children's confidence grew as their designs took shape.

They became more enthusiastic about working independently and more confident in discussing each other's work. They remained anxious, however, about sharing their work with adults.

Motivation and independence

- *Tentative responses* to the collection, with some giggling and apprehension.
- *Uncertainty* about working with unfamiliar material and without instructions or a pattern.
- *Developing enthusiasm* as they selected fabric, particularly fur and velvet.
- *Constant reassurance* and guidance needed (by some children).
- *Reluctance* to share work with other staff members.

Personal interest

- 'I love this little, soft, white bear, but there is no white fur in the suitcase.'
- 'I like this big bear, but my bear needs to be small. How do I do that?'
- 'Mine won't look like a real bear!'

Ownership

The children were embarrassed at the start, but their interest in the bears grew as the work progressed.

- 'My bear will have clothes. I shall have to design those as well.'
- 'I like putting all the things (resources) into the plastic wallet.'
- 'I like my bear, but Jane might think it's scruffy.'

The children became gradually attached to their bears and saw the link between the designs and the emerging bears. They never lost their concern about the teacher's reaction to their work.

Knowledge, skills and understanding

Tim was very tentative but was ably supported by three children.

- 'Normally Jane [the teacher] tells us what to do. I'm rubbish at making.'
- 'Do we have to design first? It's going to take too long.'
- 'I can't draw and I can't design.'

Figure 3.2 'I think that my bear looks like my design.'
Katie Jane, aged 9 years

Most of the children understood the concept of designing before making and, once started, they produced challenging and interesting paper patterns.

There was no use of colour in the children's designs, which was in line with their previous experience of designing.

There was some very good manipulation of tools and ingenious solving of problems, such as sewing on buttons.

One child remarked, 'Jane [the teacher] really won't like this because I've gone wrong.'

The children had previous knowledge of cutting, sewing and joining fabric. Their initial tentativeness was caused by the lack of definition for the project. They were very concerned about the outcome of their work and how it would be received.

Evaluation of a bear design: Rebecca, aged 10 years

> *Observer:* What was the best thing about making your bear?
> *Rebecca:* Choosing all the things.
> *Observer:* Did your bear turn out the way you wanted it to?

Rebecca:	Well it was a bit too small and it was very difficult to put his clothes on.
Observer:	Did you learn anything by making your bear?
Rebecca:	When you design by yourself you can make what you like. I like that. Does mine look like a bear?
Observer:	It does look like your design. Did you enjoy this project?
Rebecca:	It was scary at first, I didn't know how to start. I don't know if Jane will like my bear?

At all times these children were wary of adult response and were unwilling to share their progress with other adults in the classroom. Jane expected children to adhere to tightly structured technical and academic processes. As a consequence some children found it very uncomfortable to be presented with an open-ended task during which they had to make independent decisions. With reference to the attribution theory for motivation, discussed by Chaplain (2000), these children, viewed as a group, showed initial evidence of *learned helplessness*. They were prepared to say that they couldn't achieve the task, because they were not given precise instructions.

The children became more motivated as their confidence grew, but they still needed constant reassurance. Most of the children had good technical skills. They found difficulty in transferring their knowledge to a task that they had to plan and organize for themselves. Perhaps most importantly, they lacked the confidence to make decisions and to work independently. This was in contrast to the children in School 1 who were very happy 'to have a go'.

The teacher

Approaching motivation and ownership

The evidence of motivation and ownership from Schools 1 and 2 is presented in scenarios where children are working on the same project but in classroom contexts where the balance between prescription and creative exploration is viewed differently by the class teachers. This, in turn, affects the level of motivation, ownership and independence experienced by the children.

Curriculum debates in other countries (Moyles 2001) have focused on the balance between the needs of the workforce and the developmental needs of children. The curriculum in England has moved towards an outcome-driven model, where adherence to a pre-planned route is valued and evidence for assessment relies on completion of tasks. The danger with going too far down this road is that individual, creative responses will be lost in a sea of conformity.

How the prescribed curriculum can be supported by meaningful learning experiences is problematic. It is subject to a range of constraints and will be, in part, determined by the preferred pedagogy of the teacher. Parker-Rees (1997) discusses the dichotomy between planning an organized curriculum and responding to the various needs of the children. Woods and Jeffrey (1996) maintain that creative teaching has survived in some schools with resulting evidence of individual and unexpected responses from children. We need to ensure that with the drive to raise standards in numeracy and literacy we do not deny children a wider view of the curriculum, and stunt the all-round development of a generation of children.

Teacher expectation and the effect on learning

The teachers, Penny and Jane, hold different views on independence and this affects their children's motivation and self-assurance. Children acquire knowledge and skills in different ways, but only achieve true confidence in using them when they have opportunities to apply them in situations where personal goals are achieved. The teaching styles, classroom organization and management, and expectations for children's performance are very different in each classroom. The levels of independence required from the children are consequently very different. Teachers' views on independence and intervention are linked to pedagogy, perceived curriculum constraints and teacher expectation (Chapter 4).

Penny: School 1

Penny knows her children very well and is able to meet their specific needs. She has not only taught the individuals in her class but also their siblings and in one case a parent. She understands the importance of covering all the elements of the National Curriculum and other national initiatives, while still valuing opportunities to develop children's individuality. She is clear that curriculum demands can be satisfied with experiences that challenge children's intuition, natural curiosity, creativity, independence and ability to solve problems. This is apparent in the brief glimpse we have of her classroom.

The children are assured that:

- decisions can be made collectively or individually;
- what they do is valued and will be evaluated against what they have done previously;
- development of skills will be achieved through initial instruction followed by practice and working through the range of problems that occur;
- being motivated, having creative ideas and using different ways of solving problems are all important for success;
- the final product will reflect their developing understanding and their success in solving problems;
- adults will support them in order to move thinking forward and encourage them to become critically reflective.

Teaching style and the children's progress

Penny believes that 'work in progress' provides a window through which evaluation of learning can be viewed. She assesses the children's initial interpretation of a task, their progress along the way and, finally, the outcome. Her children are encouraged to reflect on their own work and thus contribute to personal assessment. Sensitive teacher/child interaction supports evaluations. Failure along the way is considered to be a part of the learning process. Teacher and children consider alternative directions and solutions. Penny is always careful to be positive, but also to help her children to reflect on their progress and to help them to make their own judgements as to possible improvements. The evaluation of the bear project, with Tom, indicates the level of genuine involvement that he has with his problem. Penny is sensitive to the children's needs and has good control of the teaching process. She is certainly aware of the educational values that must inform her teaching but she never loses sight of 'pupil cultures' (Woods and Jeffrey 1996: 14). Her teaching style is balanced (Moyles 1992). It has elements of McNamara's teacher-centred approach when, at times, she establishes full responsibility for delivering aspects of knowledge or particular skills. She does, however, value children as individuals and encourages them to make decisions and to contribute personal viewpoints. Above all, Penny is tuned in to children and uses their experiences outside school as starting points for learning. She adopts a tentative approach with the children and asks them genuine questions that elicit thoughtful and informative answers. The art of communication, described in Chapter 2, is best served by the ability of teachers to be humble and to listen to children. Some of the children in School 1 were reluctant to leave the project. They choroused, 'But when can we finish our bears?'

Context

The classroom has:

- classroom walls that hold a variety of information including word banks, alphabets devised by the children, material to explain classroom objectives to parents and questions for the children that remind them of their overall commitments for the week;
- displays that are interactive, not yet completed and directly relevant to work in progress;
- portfolios of work that are accessible to children and that they are proud to show to visitors;
- a plentiful collection of improvised resources and other materials available for use at most times of the day.

Children are encouraged to use personal possessions at various times of the day, most particularly in the playground.

Jane: School 2

Jane is an 'artist' and exerts her personal artistic control over children's work. She requires strict adherence to the requirements for a task and requires prescribed outcomes from the children. The classroom wall displays provide evidence of neatly presented work of high technical quality and uniformity of outcome. Jane transmits her preferred style to children rather than allowing them to develop their own creative vision.

Teaching style and the children's progress

In Jane's class the children have very specific expectations placed upon them. Skills are well taught. Jane's approach is 'safe' and outcomes are easy to evaluate against a class norm. Children are clear about her expectations and she ensures that the standard of their work meets her criteria. During the bear design project the children lacked confidence and initially found the task bewildering. Jane's teaching style does not encourage original ideas or open-ended problem solving. In conversation she admitted that she felt that the children should have been more closely directed during the project. She would have liked to see an emphasis on taught skills and the opportunity for children to interpret a design given to them. However, she was interested to observe the children using a range of applicable skills and solving problems, after their initial tentativeness. The children relaxed as they worked, but in spite of seeming to enjoy the task said nothing about taking the bears home. They worried continually about what their bears looked like and how they compared with the bears that belonged to their peers.

Context

The classroom has:

- portfolios that track children's work throughout the year to which children have limited access;
- displays of work that are changed regularly and demonstrate a well-organized, varied curriculum input and carefully taught skills;
- resources that are plentiful and accessible but only used under supervision and for prescribed tasks.

Children are discouraged from bringing personal possessions to school.

Conclusion

In this chapter the importance of maintaining children's intrinsic motivation has been highlighted. Children's confidence is fragile and demotivation takes place where self-esteem has been damaged and children perceive themselves to be failures. Teachers' pedagogy has an effect on the learning process and on children's views of their potential as learners. It is valuable to reflect on practice and to monitor children's attitudes to aspects of the teaching and learning experience. Motivated children working in secure but challenging classroom contexts are most likely to show a high level of independence and perseverance.

Questions about motivation include:

1 What do you feel like when you are motivated?
2 How do you know that children are interested in tasks?
3 How do your children solve problems?
4 Can your children transfer skills from one task to another?
5 Are children willing to evaluate their work and to accept advice?
6 Do children offer help to one another?
7 Do you encourage children to contribute experiences out of school to complement and extend the curriculum?

4

Classroom environments: familiar views, inspiration and implications for independence

Cameo 1

Two 10-year-olds are talking to an adult about their classroom and the playground.

Adult: What do you enjoy about your classroom?

James: We can learn things and be with our friends. We like Sally, our teacher, and Sally likes us.

Adult: Do you make changes to your classroom?

Samantha: We tell Sally where we want to put things and we change the furniture sometimes.

Adult: Can you find things in this classroom?

James: Yeh, we get our things out and we can always find the tape and the sharp scissors. All the paints and pencils and things have to be put back properly and we do all the washing up.

Adult: Can you talk to your friends?

Samantha: Sally lets us talk when we are working if she's not talking. We've got a settee in the corner and we take turns to sit there and then we can talk, but sometimes the boys get there first!

James: We talk about the playground a lot. We've got a sandpit and a willow cage and a den in the trees.

Adult: What happens at lunchtime?

Samantha: There are seats and we can be with our friends. The classes take it in turn to play with the little ones. I like the sandpit and the picnic benches. There's a friendship stop. It's a seat where you can sit if you haven't got a friend.

| | **Cameo 2**
| | The children are 10 and 11 years old. They congregate in the playground and enter the classroom when the bell goes. The date and instructions for independent literacy work are on the board. The literacy hour follows registration. A poem about the weather is shared and the teacher gives out work books. The task is to write a poem about the weather and to include examples of personification. The teacher monitors the children and moves around the tables during twenty minutes of near silence. The level of concentration is varied and during the plenary session, when the children share their work, it is clear that some have misunderstood the task. At 10.15 a.m. the children move to the hall for an assembly followed by twenty minutes in the playground. They return to the classroom for an hour of numeracy. The weekly timetable shows a tightly organized curriculum programme with clearly demarcated subject experiences.

| | **Cameo 3**
| | Four-year-old children sit on the carpet, while the teacher explains the programme for the day. The classroom is organized into work bays with carefully organized and labelled resources. On the walls there is range of complex and very bold displays. The children move from the carpet to start the tasks allocated to them. Two groups sit with work sheets while children in a third group adopt roles in a travel agency. A fourth group is making geometric, three-dimensional forms using plastic construction material.

Introduction

Learning environments, as well as the influences that have shaped and continue to shape them, are investigated in this chapter. Alexander (2000: 533) reflects on educational ideas and practice as having 'migrated from one culture to another'. His research highlights the similarities and differences found in the education systems in five countries. In India, Russia, and sometimes in France children face the blackboard with a teaching focus characterized as *unitary* and an emphasis on *work*. Children in England, parts of the USA and sometimes in France are more commonly organized into groups, described as *multiple-focus*. The characteristic English classroom was found to 'hover' between providing for *work* and acknowledging *pleasure*.

Provision for interactive learning stems from the work of Piaget. Vygotsky and Bruner promoted the view that interactive learning takes place in social settings. The Board of Education Consultative Committee under Hadow (Board of Education 1931) and the Plowden Report (CACE 1967) promoted enthusiasm for children to learn through active, first-hand experience. However, concern arose that the holistic view of the child and education appeared not to have worked (Sylva 2001). The 1988 Education Reform Act called for a return to basics and a move towards a more traditional subject-based approach. The requirement for teachers to be skilled in using whole-class teaching methods as well as collaborative group work and individual interaction with children stems from the influential discussion paper by Alexander *et al.* (1992). The National Literacy Strategy (DfEE 1998) has introduced a new way to structure an hour using whole-class, group and independent approaches. The thrust of education has moved through a period of valuing the process of learning to a concentration on curriculum outcomes and the achievement of satisfactory scores in tests.

The generic term *environment* refers to the physical learning space and to the people and ideas that contribute to learning. The *framework* for the environment – space, pupil organization, time, content, routine, rule and ritual – reflects the school ethos and wider societal issues (Alexander 2000). The organizational strategies that teachers bring to the curriculum and the interpersonal relationship between adults and children will have a lasting effect on children's learning. Overarching policies from central and local government and the perceived constraints that result must be tackled with confidence and firmness, when establishing what is appropriate for children. A learning environment that promotes independence will provide a framework for children's developing self-esteem and responsibility. With an affective climate and mutual concern for well-being, teachers and children will be better prepared to achieve personal and national targets. Alexander sees a national and international need to reshape primary education for a changing world. In order to influence any change, teachers need to reflect on the environment that they are providing for children's learning and to ask questions such as Why, What for, For whose benefit, and Are there changes that can be made?

The context

In Cameo 1 children had played a part in sensitive modification of their indoor and outdoor environment. The children show responsibility for one another and for their work place. Cameo 2 introduces a classroom where children are passive learners with no requirement to show independence or originality. In Cameo 3 the presentation of an orderly, well-resourced classroom conceals the reality of controlled classroom practice and restriction on use of the resources. The learning environments have superficial similarities, but the differences in teachers' pedagogy cause differences in the emphasis placed on aspects of organization and attitudes towards children.

As we have seen in Chapter 3, classroom organization and management have an effect on children's motivation and independence. Moyles (1992) explains that the physical environment provides constraints as well as opportunities. If we agree that organization for education needs to provide for aspects of learning that are broader than the prescribed curriculum, then the starting point should be a review and evaluation of learning provision. In this way teachers will find out how the classroom climate contributes to children's development and how it contributes to an understanding of what inspires and motivates children.

Teachers, in spite of their prior enthusiasm, experience and skills, have 'a daily struggle to reconcile differing expectations about what they should and should not do' (Alexander 2000: 196). With pressure on children to achieve specific outcomes, the familiar view of daily organization might be obscuring significant underlying changes in aims and objectives for teaching and learning. The style and layout of the classroom in Cameo 3 is hiding the reality of the style adopted for teaching and learning. The daily organization for learning is not necessarily reflected in the organization of physical space.

Starting from what is familiar

It is important to start with what we understand by a climate for learning. Supposing that we were asked to explain familiar patterns of English primary classroom organization and management to a teacher from rural Africa. We would need to think

Figure 4.1 A primary classroom in Malawi in Central Africa

about what has influenced the way English classrooms are organized, why the day is structured in a particular way and what the origin is of the 'stuff' in classrooms.

The following questions highlight issues for an evaluation of learning environments.

1 What influences the way in which the learning environment is organized?
2 How are affective, social and creative considerations provided for in classrooms?
3 How could the environment provide more cognitive challenge for children?

Figure 4.2 What has influenced the way English classrooms are organized?

Figure 4.3 Who decides what 'stuff' will be stored in the classroom?

4 How does the environment reflect children's experiences outside school?
5 How much evidence is there of global issues and important cultural influences on children's lives?
6 Are children asked to discuss their feelings about the environment and to contribute to change?
7 How does the environment provide for an independent approach to learning?
8 Do curriculum pressures result in compromise for children's development?
9 Where can inspiration for change be found?

Alexander, Rose and Woodhead (1992: 38), the so-called Three Wise Men, suggested that 'pupils should encounter a purposeful and orderly classroom that encourages a high level of interest'. To achieve purpose, order and interest requires teachers to understand the relationship between development and learning, to listen to children and hear what they say and to shape an environment, with them, that ensures mutual trust and respect. The national requirements for the curriculum will be achieved more comfortably in well-managed learning environments where intrinsic motivation is encouraged through independence and responsibility.

Teachers and children can monitor provision through a simple but ongoing audit of the environment in which they share their learning.

A classroom audit should start with a consideration of what has influenced practice in classrooms

The beliefs and values of teachers are the primary influences on the way classrooms are organized and managed. These beliefs have been shaped by:

- cultural and educational experiences;
- the ethos and climate of the school;
- an understanding of the values and aspirations that children bring to school;
- national legislation, initiatives and local trends;
- the expectations that teachers have for children in their care;
- the characteristics of the micro-culture of the classroom;
- views on traditional patterns for classrooms for 4–11-year-olds.

Some teachers use an instructional or expositional style of delivery. They may regularly direct children's learning (Cameos 2 and 3), and this will be reflected in the organization of the classroom. On the other hand, primary classrooms may be seen as places where interactive and collaborative teaching takes place and where organization of furniture, resources and the structure of the day provide opportunities for teaching individuals, groups and the whole class. However, even where classrooms appear to support this pedagogical style there may be significant organizational and ethical differences. Teachers' pedagogy or their 'preference, personal characteristics and teaching styles' will be diverse (Pointon and Kershner 2001: 55). The culture and climate of the school will alter over time but changes in legislation and the introduction of initiatives must not be allowed to have an adverse effect on established good practice. It is important for teachers to take a closer look at what is really happening in their classrooms and to take time to do an audit.

Framework for a classroom audit

Daily organization

Children in classrooms throughout England will be given varying opportunities for:

- receiving formal and integrated approaches to teaching and learning;
- moving from whole-class and whole-school activities to small group and interactive 'workshop' situations;
- moving out of doors for different purposes and periods of time;
- spending time alone;
- talking, being listened to, playing, making choices and taking responsibility;
- innovation or independence;
- contribution of ideas and demonstration of skills.

Aspects of the daily organization for teaching and learning will provide children with a variety of opportunities for independence. The observable differences in provision are not as important as the actual quality of interaction between adults and children and their shared attitudes.

Questions for teachers

1 What are the positive aspects of the daily organization of the classroom?
2 Which aspects of daily organization need modification in order to allow children more opportunity to think and to respond independently?
3 Are the subject-oriented learning bays really used for interactive, cooperative investigation?
4 Is the 'carpet' sometimes a refuge for children to read quietly, or is it always used as the position for didactic teacher-led exposition?
5 Are children encouraged to talk about their lives outside the school and to contribute their knowledge to the curriculum?
6 What are the criteria for grouping children? Is there any flexibility in the composition of the groups?

Physical space

The space, in primary classrooms, is normally organized with furniture appropriate for children's use and for storage. Commercial and improvised resources and materials are stored in a variety of ways, both visible and concealed. Areas of the classroom may be designated for particular 'subjects' or styles of learning with a settee for a quiet chat, or a carpet for interactive whole-class teaching. A bird's eye view of classrooms should provide a relief map of the probable curriculum and an impression of the approach to teaching and learning (Moyles 1995). This will not be true in all classrooms. Space that is well organized (Cameo 3) does not always reveal the reality of its use. Perceived curriculum constraints have caused a less interactive use of classroom space, and the opportunities that children have to operate creatively, spontaneously and independently have been curtailed.

Questions for teachers

1 Which areas of your classroom are used effectively?
2 Are there areas of the classroom that are underused or poorly used?
3 How does the current organization of space encourage children to be independent and responsible?

4 If you intend to make changes to the physical environment how can children be involved in decision making?

There is normally a subtle and gradual change in the interactive approach to classroom planning and organization as children move from the Reception class through Key Stage 1 and into Key Stage 2. By the time children are at the end of the primary age phase the view of the presentation of classrooms may have become dramatically modified and will possibly resemble the more austere secondary school model. Does this have to preclude children having interactive experiences and opportunities for decision making? This theme is returned to in Chapters 5 and 6.

Displays

Displays determine the way the classroom looks and make a distinct impression on children and adults (Moyles 1992). Displays cover walls and surfaces, especially in classrooms for the younger children. They have a variety of functions including the celebration of children's achievements, reminders of learning strategies (mathematical tables or word banks), sharing of topic-related materials and reminders to children of standards for behaviour and rules for managing resources. The quality, style and purpose of displays will be determined by some of the influences determined at the start of the chapter. These include teachers' cultural expectations, as well as their educational experiences, expertise and expectations.

Displays will also be influenced by adult ideas about aesthetics and style of presentation. These will be determined by the culture and climate of the school, as well as by the preference of teachers. The influences will provide determining factors in the choice and use of display materials. Many schools have an 'in-house style' that may involve hours of preparation, with prestige gained by those who achieve the ideal. Although the organization of displays may not be optional for teachers it is important to stop, look and listen!

Questions for teachers

1 What purposes are served by displays?
2 Could displays make a more efficient and realistic contribution to learning?

3 Is there an approach to display that will provide a more sensitive, interactive and informative advertisement for the whole
curriculum?
4 How can displays reflect the cultural experience of children?
5 Who decides what will be displayed?
6 How can children be given encouragement to make independent displays that include aspects of life outside school?
7 Do we understand that not everybody will appreciate a
particular style of display?
8 How much time is spent in the organisation of displays? Is this
time well spent?

Resources

Resources are intended to support learning and give children the
chance to interact with a range of commercial and improvised
artefacts. With the youngest children, resources should be selected
that allow continuing exploration, investigation and discovery
(Fisher 1996: 66). Older children, however, have no less need to
continue to be curious, independent, creative and intellectually
stimulated through recourse to well-chosen materials. Fisher highlights 'building blocks' as expensive but essential resources that
provide a foundation for learning across curriculum areas. Improvised resources will possibly be relevant to children's experiences outside school or they may provide new experiences that can
be followed up in future leisure time. In Chapter 6 this theme is
developed. With an eye on both commercial and non-commercial
resources there are principles for collecting and organizing materials that help children to learn effectively. They include the
relevance of resources for the many facets of learning and for
the creative connections that should be possible if resources are
carefully chosen.

Questions for teachers

1 Were the resources inherited?
2 What is the rationale for selecting additional resources?
3 What evidence do you have that the resources provide
challenge?
4 How can resources help children to develop cognitive
understanding?

5 Do the resources have a gender bias?
6 Do the resources reflect diversity of home experience on either a temporary or a permanent basis?
7 How can resources reflect the experiences of children with particular needs?
8 Are resources discussed with children and are their opinions sought about any additions?
9 Do resources reflect the personal interests and areas of expertise of the adults?

Well-chosen resources do not need to be associated with specific subject objectives. The best resources provide a wealth of opportunities for a range of curriculum areas. Building blocks can be as useful with 11-year-olds as with the youngest children. Resources with flexible possibilities should be available for creative and inventive use by children across the 4–11 age range. Exploration, investigation and discovery should continue on a regular basis with older children. Too often the curriculum is prescribed and the pedagogy does not allow for reflection on the possibilities afforded by a range of 'stuff'. Pollard (1997: 218) discusses '. . . the importance of direct experience and practical work for children's learning'. Cameo 2 presents a narrow organizational model of teaching and learning, where direction and prescription, in a limited environment, are seen as the expedient strategies for achieving particular academic outcomes. Cameo 1, on the other hand, provides a glimpse of 'bringing the outside inside', with discussion of the sandpit in the playground and the use of dens and a willow cage. The possibilities for an independent approach to learning afforded in this environment are developed in the following chapters.

A ruthless review of resources can help to make the learning environment more challenging and educationally viable

1 Gather all the resources together and discuss with children and colleagues which to keep, which to store centrally, which to add to and which to discard.
2 Decide on the criteria to be used when selecting additional, generic resources as well as particular resources that support current initiatives.

3 Discuss aspects of children's experience that are not being addressed through the resource collection.
4 Which are the most effective resources for supporting children's independent learning? What additions could be made?
5 Which resources support children who have particular educational needs?
6 Which resources are a 'waste of space'?
7 How much use is made of resources that come from the local or the natural environment?
8 How well is children's culture, including popular culture, reflected in the resources provided or introduced on a temporary basis?
9 Are children encouraged to discuss interesting items and are they allowed to contribute resources to complement religious or cultural interests?

View expensive commercial resources with caution

When looking at glossy catalogues consider the following questions.

1 Will a chosen resource be useful for a *range* of learning opportunities?
   Example: clay, blocks, a range of pens, pencils, pastels, well-chosen computer software.
2 Could the resource chosen be replicated by using improvised materials?
   Example: collections of natural materials can substitute for bags of plastic counting materials.
3 Could requests to parents and children yield a wealth of durable, relevant and flexible resources?
   Examples: one or two 'McDonald's toys' brought from a child's home will multiply into a flexible collection if all children are encouraged to follow suit. A temporary collection of mechanical toys from home will provide excellent material for a project on *How Things Work.*

Suschitzky and Chapman (1998: 67) suggest that 'materials and resources, provided in the school, should reflect and extend the children's backgrounds and experiences'. A constraint on this proposal will be the size of the class. Appropriate provision of resources will reflect commonalities as well as differences in children's experiences and provide a broader perspective on the world. Creating effective learning environments presents teachers and children with a challenge. When implementing change it is important to believe that:

- perceived constraints on organization and resourcing can be viewed positively;
- flexibility, responsibility and independent action will be key aspects of the long-term and day-to-day organization of the environment;
- children should have some responsibility for organization, decision making and evaluation of classroom organization;
- children need to have opportunities to contribute ideas and resources and to explore the commonalities of their experience rather than the differences.

The teacher

National innovation has been almost as powerful an influence on the curriculum as legislation. Local innovation and trends have also always been a source of local excitement and subsequent classroom changes. The problem is what Robinson, cited in Galton (1989), says is the numbing effect on teachers of numerous changes that have lacked prior evaluation. Trends, 'fads' and local requirements for 'moving forward' have long been an influence on schools. Many of these disappear without trace but some remain to become important influences on the fabric of classroom organization. The High/Scope approach to the curriculum has given us important elements for 'planning, doing and reviewing' and general organization. The Steiner and Montessori philosophies have left lasting influences on the early years curriculum. The Reggio Emilia approach to education, in northern Italy, has a long history of success with organization for learning that takes the development of children into account and advocates adult involvement that is rigorous in its learning aims but tentative in its forward planning. Aspects of the Reggio Emilia approach as well as the High/Scope curriculum are discussed in Chapter 5. The numeracy and literacy strategies in England have also had a profound effect on the structure and organization of the classroom environment.

Changes in classrooms: revised approaches to organization for learning

Change is beneficial when it allows for a better response to the particular needs of a group of children and where children's views have been sought (Kershner 2000). The strong legacy left from a child-centred view of education should surely be used as a foundation on which to build additional educational requirements for children in the twenty-first century. It must not be superseded by a curriculum that denies children opportunities to develop personal, creative and independent responses. Moyles (1992) discusses the influence of teachers' beliefs on classroom organization and experiences. Fisher (1996) discusses the effective use of space and resources as having an effect on children's independence. When considering a broadening of educational experience and ways of building on the excellent practice that survives in many of our classrooms, it is practical to consider what changes are necessary and how effective change will be inspired by more creative curriculum practice. Change should not be forced upon teachers but should allow them to recognize:

- a need for modification of approach to organization and interaction between children;
- the need to feel comfortable with new ideas and to have confidence in integrating them into their current effective practice;
- the need to reflect on previous experience and to internalize ideas from reading and research that complement the need for autonomy and independence.

The survey teachers saw younger children as needing:

- an imaginative and creative approach to learning;
- practical experience in order to establish meaning;
- a chance to hypothesize and to get quick reassurance, adult support, and answers to questions;
- clarification of the objective for the activity as often as needed;
- open-ended and challenging tasks;
- adult encouragement when tasks are proving to be difficult.

Some of the survey teachers saw young children as being forced to be 'independent' or working in isolation before they were developmentally ready to understand why they could no longer interact with adults.

Can teachers provide a learning environment suited to all children?

'*Learning across the National Curriculum*' (DfEE/QCA 1999: 19–22) is a section of the National Curriculum framework that includes wide-ranging, affective, social, moral and reflective attributes that need to be developed. These aspects of learning require flexibility of approach and a clear understanding of children's development. Reassurance is provided for teachers who want to broaden their curriculum perspective. It is important to support children's learning with a wider socio-cultural commitment. The initiatives and trends that need to be incorporated into classroom practice should be complemented by developmentally appropriate experience. They provide an opportunity to refocus the direction of teaching and enrich rather than deplete experience. Changes in educational direction should encourage teachers to revitalize the environment. Inspiration for modifying learning environments and teaching strategies is addressed in the chapters that follow.

The teachers in the survey group were generally positive about the need for an independent approach in the classroom. The discussion became more negative, however, as some teachers talked about the influence that the Literacy Strategy had had on their practice as well as on the classroom environment. The survey teachers saw independence in the Literacy Hour as requiring children to:

- work alone or in isolation;
- work at tasks that have been directed by the teacher and that have to be completed in a set time;
- work without support or the chance to ask questions at the time when the answer is needed;
- work without recourse to additional resources and information;
- work quietly without disturbing the teacher.

These teachers also saw a tendency for children to be engaged in low-level activities. They mentioned children:

- not understanding or misinterpreting the task;
- given closed, limited, menial tasks;
- involved in too much recapping and little challenge;
- given very explicit instructions that restrict options and creative responses;
- copying their peers;

- experiencing over-reliance on work sheets and narrowly based commercial or in-house material.

Responses from teachers of older children were more positive. They indicated similar problems, but they:

- acknowledged children's growing independence as they moved through the junior school;
- pointed out that able children showed increased motivation when given clear targets and a short time scale;
- valued the chance for teachers to provide well-designed tasks that children can work on, return to and complete by the end of the week;
- showed an awareness of the children who are able to understand the value of working unaided and taking responsibility for their learning;
- appreciated the value of encouraging children to take risks and to use a wide range of accessible resources;
- acknowledged the strength of peer support;
- valued the opportunity for teachers to focus on one group while other children work independently.

It was felt by teachers of older children that with sufficient training both children and adults could make this version of independence work. The general feeling, however, was that young children needed experience of an independent approach to learning in its broadest sense. They would then be more able to exercise the self-discipline necessary to focus on prescribed tasks without adult support.

Teachers and pedagogy

Teachers who value an environment that supports independence have to arrive at an appropriate pedagogy, and this causes confusion (Moyles 1992). The National Curriculum and the more recent *Curriculum Guidance for the Foundation Stage* (DfEE/QCA 2000) have provided information on what to teach or at least what the outcomes of teaching should be. The best ways of achieving these outcomes are still largely left to the integrity of the teacher and the school's preferred model for delivering the curriculum. Moyles discusses the dilemma faced by teachers in balancing their perceived need to control curriculum delivery with an approach that acknowledges children's right to access the 'hidden curriculum'. How to make space, time and opportunities to incorporate children's ideas and experiences provides a challenge for teachers. If the entitlement for all children is to achieve their potential, then teachers need to reflect on whether they are delivering what Nieto, cited in Collins *et al.* (2001), describes as regurgitated and passively accepted knowledge or a curriculum that values children's prior experience.

The child

Teachers should be able to maintain a stable approach to teaching and learning and to build on what they know about children. They need to be able to develop an approach that takes into account the importance of interaction with individuals and to maintain respect and opportunity for children's cognitive, linguistic and social contributions. When working towards the requirements for legislated curriculum and additional initiatives, Alexander *et al.* (1992) see the need to strike the balance and consider fitness for purpose.

The Plowden Report (CACE 1967) had an important influence on educational debate. Children were placed at the centre of the education system and there was a limited blossoming of 'progressive education'. Galton (1989) described the report as distinctive, powerful and comprehensive. Its strength lay in relating the curriculum to children's psychological development and to gathering evidence from national surveys. The principles for teaching advocated by the report were not, however, generally implemented. This lay partly in the false premise that all children are inherently virtuous, curious and keen to learn (Galton 1989). Little support was given to teachers to help them to differentiate between the aspects of the Plowden principles that were desirable and efficient and those that were impractical. For many teachers, working with children in the 1960s was a rewarding and energizing experience. With teachers of older children, however, there was some uncertainty and guilt when they realized that they were required to listen to children's ideas and take their interests into account. Teachers were offered a creative direction for curriculum delivery that suited neither their training and experience nor the perceived practicalities and constraints that faced them in the classroom. The climate at the time became characterized as being full of pressures, imperatives, 'no go areas', relaxation of subject boundaries, a laissez-faire attitude and teachers in perpetual motion. There was limited truth in such extreme views.

Pollard (1996) comments on the need for children to experience classrooms that reflect the cultural understanding that they bring with them. Pollard (1997: 35) suggests that people experience 'interplay of social forces and individual actions'. He further reflects that any decisions that we make in our lives are regulated by societal structure and various constraints, but our capacity for individual thought and action serves to develop new understanding that helps to shape cultures and to effect change.

If children are encouraged to present their views on classrooms (Fisher 1996), it is likely that environments will be created that have meaning for them. Moyles (1992: 35) says that children must '. . . share intentions and requisite strategies for access and retrieval (of materials)'. Children need to learn collaboratively, to view issues from a variety of perspectives and be curious, questioning and active problem solvers. Teachers who aspire to educate the whole child will assert that children are entitled to have their individual needs recognized. The consideration of individual children's needs has to be reconciled with the need to satisfy curriculum outcomes. In the previous chapters the importance of self-esteem was seen as integral to the themes of communication and motivation. Pollard sees learning as taking place in a socio-cultural approach where there are links between thought and language, culture, history and self-identity (Collins *et al.* 2001). Most teachers operate within a traditional organizational structure with an easily recognizable classroom layout. Teachers' intuitive and established views of learning should be reflected in this model. The way forward is to consider the management and organizational requirements for a broad-based curriculum that takes into account the needs of *all* children and reflects the shifting and changing educational and political stances that are a part of educational requirement.

Conclusion

In this chapter there is a strong recommendation for teachers to audit their environmental provision and to work with children and other adults to make joint decisions about appropriate changes. The issue of independence is embedded in the suggestions for carrying out the audit. Evidence from the group of survey teachers indicates that recent changes in educational direction have left them confused and uncertain about the way forward. This is typical of the adjustment that has always been required of teachers. The response to change should, however, stem from a foundation of appropriate developmental understanding and an enthusiasm for modification and development.

5

Independence in practice: inspiration for change

Cameo 1

In a school in the northern Italian town of Reggio Emilia, two 6-year-old boys are working in a private space. They are building a castle using a collection of small building blocks and related junk material. They offer each other suggestions for modifications.

The boundaries to the working space are formed on three sides by a window, a wall and a long, low cupboard over which it is possible for adults to observe. A temporary projection screen provides a final flexible boundary. The children have privacy without isolation and are able to leave this personal space by crawling under the screen. A slide projector, on the cupboard, runs a continuous slide loop of slide images showing piazzas, churches, castles and markets. On the temporary screen, the children project drawings on overhead transparencies to show their 'work in progress' and to revisit aspects of their designs. An *educator* (teacher) looks over the cupboard and suggests another source of building materials to the children.

The castle the children are building is a contribution to a group project on castles and bridges. Children in the 'mini atelier' (art workshop) are working at the same time on a clay landscape with a castle and a bridge.

Cameo 2

In Polly's class there is a gentle start to the day. 9- and 10-year-old children relax with books and comics and talk about toys brought from home, while parents speak to Polly.

Polly goes to the group and greets them with 'Guten Morgen'. The children respond to their names during registration with 'Guten Morgen, Polly.' Moses, the 'special person' for the day, takes the completed register to the office. Polly speaks to the group. 'It is good to see you reading, you seem to really enjoy books. Sam, please can you tell us a little bit about the tiny football figures you have brought to school?'

The numeracy lesson starts with a discussion of number bonds. The use of the inverse process for checking calculations is revisited. The children working with Polly have acknowledged that they have not grasped the concept. They do not understand that the answer to the algorithm $24-11=13$ can be checked using the inverse algorithm $11+13$, giving the answer 24. After discussion Polly asks the more confident children to check their understanding with algorithms to 10 and then help those children who are still unsure.

Cameo 3

Two 4-year-olds are mixing their own colours and painting with tiny brushes. One 3-year-old child paints alone. She has to move round the table to access the paint and water. The older children had set up the materials and the younger child joined the activity later. One of the older children looks at the little girl's painting and says, 'It's very messy, isn't it, but she's only little.' Karen, the teacher, moves to the group and discusses the way in which painting skills develop.

Introduction

In this chapter there is an attempt to understand how independent attitudes to teaching and learning evolve and how they can be nurtured, maintained and stimulated. The three cameos show children working within learning frameworks based on respect for children and understanding of social and emotional as well as cognitive development. In Cameo 1 children are working independently and creatively. They are contributing to a group theme, working as a pair and extending their existing knowledge and understanding. The curriculum framework is based on the Reggio Emilia approach to teaching and learning (discussed in this chapter). Cameo 2 provides a glimpse of classroom interaction that is rooted in an inclusive approach to education where the importance of responsibility for one another is very strong.

In Cameo 3 the curriculum framework is based on the High/ Scope approach (discussed in this chapter). The children are observed during 'work time'. As the children talk, Karen is able to intervene sensitively to support their discussion and introduce them to ideas about the gradual development of skills and understanding. Although the adults are playing slightly different roles in each cameo, their intentions are similar. The ownership of learning is with the children. Adults are observing, guiding, extending existing knowledge and contributing new concepts and ideas.

As children get older the pressure of the curriculum increases and the demand for accountability becomes greater. Curriculum delivery may be didactic. Tensions inevitably exist and Cullingford (1990: 181) describes a 'major problem for teachers being . . . the conflict between what they would like to do and the realities of the classroom'. Where pedagogy is based on an understanding of children's development, teachers are serious about achieving a breadth of education. Inspiration is taken from a range of sources and children are given time to develop knowledge, skills and understanding.

Ofsted (1993: 1) looked at the variety of influences on the extent and rate of children's learning and the importance of 'the quality of classroom management'. Sammons *et al.* (1995: 21), when talking about raising children's self-esteem, saw the attitude of teachers towards children as being of paramount importance. Respecting and understanding children, responding to personal needs and communicating enthusiasm were seen as having 'a beneficial influence on outcomes'.

Aspects of the Reggio Emilia approach, the High/Scope curriculum and a curriculum based on an inclusive approach to education are discussed in this chapter. No curriculum approach can be adopted in its entirety, but it is hoped that elements of each will provide inspiration for change.

The teacher

Pedagogy encompasses theories, beliefs and policies. Effective pedagogy requires a sympathetic interpretation of influences and pressures, in order to ensure that relationships between teachers and children are positive (Alexander 2000). Acceptance of a particular philosophy will not necessarily lead to an independent approach to teaching and learning. Teachers develop a personal pedagogy that inevitably accommodates their prior experience and the realities of life in classrooms. A strong educational philosophy provides a foundation for teaching and learning. Opportunities still exist, however, for modification to help to neutralize curriculum constraints, challenge anomalies and increase children's sensitive interaction within classrooms. Practice may be influenced by knowledge of alternative educational experiences. Vecchi (1998: 128) talks of research findings as becoming 'a source of energy for changing the present and orienting the future'. There is, however, a 'health warning' attached to any attempt to emulate practice from other cultures and countries. The English education system has strong traditions that need rescuing and teachers need to maintain confidence in what they already know about teaching and learning. Teachers need to adopt aspects of inspirational practice that complement and extend their existing practice.

Promoting independence in classrooms

The teachers who took part in the survey provided strong ideas about the value that they placed on independence. In Chapter 4, however, evidence from the same survey suggested that the structure of the Literacy Hour had caused teachers to lose confidence in promoting independence. Encouraging and developing independence requires teachers to believe that children can be active, responsible learners, and to have confidence in establishing a regime in which the curriculum is followed within a positive climate which fosters independence. Curriculum demands should not inhibit the development of children's inherent desire to act for themselves and take responsibility for others. The survey teachers discussed the following question: 'How do you encourage the development of independence in your teaching situation?'

The teachers saw the importance of:

- encouraging children to select and use a range of resources;
- giving children genuine responsibility throughout the day;
- children taking messages;
- giving children clear objectives and allowing them to judge when they are ready to move on;

- valuing children's work achieved through independent action;
- encouraging a creative approach to problem solving;
- encouraging peer support;
- providing models and frameworks to support investigation rather than only supplying answers;
- allowing children to try things out and to make mistakes;
- providing tasks that benefit from a degree of independent work;
- helping children to develop action plans to organize their time;
- using clear questions and explanations so that children can adopt similar techniques;
- allowing time for talk and for expression of views and concerns;
- introducing strategies for organizing finished and unfinished work;
- having a fair policy for behaviour that encourages children to be responsible for their actions;
- encouraging children to be involved in planning and assessing their own learning;
- helping children to understand that there will be times of teacher unavailability.

The child

Fisher (1996: 76) considers the value of creating an environment for learning where children's feelings are respected, where adults and children talk together and where time is spent helping children to establish an independent approach to learning. Children are sensitive to their surroundings and very aware that the school environment will be one in which they may 'fail'. Children often experience shame and embarrassment when they are put in situations where there is no time to reflect on previous knowledge to help with resolving problems. This is especially true in a climate where the teacher always seeks the right answer (Holt, cited in Pollard and Bourne 1994).

The children in the classroom cameos appear to value themselves and to see themselves as learners. They are comfortable about their position as members of their particular group and show respect for one another. Merry (1998: 79) discusses the progress that is made towards gaining self-esteem. His terminology provides a useful framework for illustrating the journey towards becoming personally confident. First, it is necessary to understand who we are by gaining a *concept of self*. The young child recognizes its mirror image at around one year of age and the concept of self develops gradually. Developing a *self-image* and establishing an *ideal self* will then result from the response to the *image of self* that children receive from other people. Establishing and maintaining self-esteem is an important part of mutual understanding between adults and children. Even after gaining *self-esteem* it is still important constantly to review *possible self* and *true self*. Self-esteem is fragile and easily destroyed. Teachers, as well as children, need constant reassurance that they are valued for the variety of contributions that they make. They should, however, have responsibility for reflection on the effect that their projection of 'self' has on others and a chance for discussion and consideration of strategies for modification and improvement.

The children in the Reggio Emilia school (Cameo 1) are working independently and purposefully. They are able to seek adult advice when necessary and respond to adult suggestions. The girls in Karen's class (Cameo 3) are able to manage their own activities and given time to consider the progress of another child. Karen moved into the group to listen and respond at an appropriate time.

Children have a variety of prior understandings of what it means to be independent (Chapter 2). Pollard (1996) says that the classroom should reflect the cultural background of the children. The cultural background of any group of children will be characterized by diversity and the classroom ethos will be shaped by realistic decisions that will inevitably involve compromise. In Cameo 2 Polly is seemingly trying to achieve a balance between the school culture and the home experiences of the children. It is made easier for her because the school culture is strongly inclusive and welcomes contributions from children and their families. She is able to interact with children and parents in a way that provides genuine respect and interest. She also encourages interaction between children that helps them to value their diverse skills and raise their personal esteem. She is able to elicit individual conceptual needs through her sensitive understanding of the children's development and through asking their opinions.

In Cameo 3 Karen's very young children are encouraged to take responsibility for their activities, seek help as appropriate and reflect verbally on the development of their work. In Cameo 1 the children work in a climate where there is a well-defined educational philosophy and confident children and adults work independently with high expectations of one another. In Cameo 2 children have responsibility for identifying their conceptual misgivings and self-select themselves into a group where they are ably supported by the teacher and given hope that 'all will be revealed!' In the three educational settings children are trusted by adults and given ownership of aspects of their learning. With each curriculum approach the children are confident that their responses will be received positively and that adults will intervene tentatively but clearly to move their learning forward.

Fisher (1996) describes schools as demonstrating a low level of independence because of the need for conformity. Many adults, however, have the motivation and inspiration to recognize when change is appropriate. As an example, a teacher may have clear views on how the class could develop thinking and problem-solving skills. The teacher will, however, need to exercise his/her value system within a system that has inevitable constraints. These constraints, whether real or perceived, are not insurmountable but they provide a challenge. Inspiration is available from alternative curriculum frameworks that take account of children's prior understanding and help to develop responsibility and shared understanding.

Sources of inspiration come in a variety of ways. Study visits abroad, attendance at conferences, approval of curriculum initiatives by respected educators, the media and particular bandwagons may provide suggestions and rationale for changes. There is a danger, however, that quick 'fixes' for educational change will be put in place without thought. Reading books, researching presentations and considering research have a further influence on practitioners. However, if the existing educational framework is insecure then introduction of new ideas may create confusion and uncertainty. There are strong educational traditions in many English schools. American and European educators were among the many visitors who flocked to see what was happening in primary education in England in the 1960s. Italian educators wanted to emulate what they saw in England and in the United States. Successful educational practice is built on an evolutionary process and cannot be simply transplanted (Edwards *et al.* 1998). What is important is to recognize the intellectual traditions of other educational frameworks. In this way teachers can consider what can be learned about approaches to children's learning and about the organization and management of other learning environments.

The Reggio Emilia approach

In Italy, at the end of the Second World War and after the restrictions of the fascist regime, the growth of reform movements, particularly the women's movement, were a feature of a national drive for improvement. Reggio Emilia is a town in the Reggio Romangna region of northern Italy. A group of parents and teachers had a vision for an innovative education system. They looked for inspiration in France and from the *progressive* movements in Britain and America (Edwards *et al.* 1998; Valentine 1999; Abbot and Nutbrown 2001). They drew on the work of Dewey, Piaget and Vygotsky to discover more about the development of children. Loris Malaguzzi, a local teacher, became interested in the movement, took time off from teaching to study psychology and became their leader. By the end of the 1970s there were 19 schools organized within the philosophy and framework of the Reggio Emilia approach.

The Reggio Emilia system has distinctive pedagogical features as well as innovative ideas for organization and management of schools. Nurseries or *nidi* for children under 3 years and schools for children between 3 and 6 years are still being developed. Parents, educators and children currently work in collaboration and schools are managed on a community basis. Cameo 1 provides a 'snapshot' of children working in a Reggio Emilia school. The approach to children's intellectual development focuses on symbolic representation. Children are encouraged to communicate and express themselves through drawing, painting, talking, dancing, sculpting, building, shadow play, working with colour and light and play-acting. These are just some of the expressive tools that have become known as 'the hundred languages of children'. Organization of the learning environment is central to the breadth and quality of learning. Space, time and resources are aspects of the organization that are considered, whatever the age of the children. The environment is conducive to children's autonomous research and discovery. Effort and attention is given to ensuring that materials, resources, space and furniture are organized to allow children easy access (Valentine 1999). The classes have 25 children and two teachers called *educatori*. There is a resident artist or *atalierista* in each school. Overall supervision of a group of schools is carried out by a *pedagogista*. The Reggio Emilia approach to education has evolved for children up to 6 years of age but there are important components of this approach to learning that would benefit the education of children across the English primary age range.

The teacher

- the *educatori* or teachers are seen as learners and develop their understanding of how children learn on a daily basis;
- time is given to the co-teachers for discussion and evaluation of the children's work and of their own contribution and the possible paths for future learning;
- a dialogue is created between all the class teachers where talents and ideas are shared;
- time is spent in forward planning based on observation of children and for the important documentation that is made readily available for parents;
- the *atelierista* is a resident artist who runs an *atelier* or creative workshop and supports the children in their project work;
- the *pedagogista* works closely, as a pedagogical adviser, with the teachers and *atelieristi* from a cluster of schools.

The emergent, organic curriculum is one that relies on close observation of children. Teachers are skilled in putting strategies into place that will extend interest and help to develop important topics. Project work may be of short- or medium-term duration or it may involve work that takes place over a very long period. Topics may be *exotic* but will more often be related to the local or immediate environment, where importance is placed on projects that are familiar to children and to which they can readily contribute. Katz observes that '. . . the children themselves can take leadership in planning and can assume responsibilities for specific observations and information and artefacts to be collected and closely examined' (Katz, cited in Edwards *et al.* 1998: 33).

In schools following the Reggio Emilia approach, importance is placed on the learning that takes place with children in group settings where they are encouraged to cooperate, collaborate and solve problems. Planning and preparation, although ongoing, are without the pressure of predetermined outcomes or activities contrived to arrive at fixed targets. Teachers have a complex supporting role and the role of parents is one of involvement without intrusion (Hendrick 1997; Valentine 1999).

Many international observers have found children in Reggio Emilia schools to be confident in their interaction with peers, adults, objects and symbolic material. Particularly significant is their ability to explore.

The context

> We place enormous value on the role of the environment as a motivating and animating force in creating spaces for relations, options and emotional and cognitive situations that produce a sense of well-being and security.
>
> (Malaguzzi 1996: 40)

Expansive and very challenging work takes place in large areas. Small-scale intricate activities are allocated smaller spaces. Ceppi and Zini (1998) see the school as a workshop for research and experimentation and as a laboratory for individual and group learning. Each school is organized in a similar way, but buildings vary from those designed by architects working in conjunction with a Reggio 'team' to villas that have been carefully adapted. The characteristic layout includes:

- a central area or piazza, where adults and children meet, work and play in a more expansive way than in the classroom;
- service areas, including the kitchen and the bathroom, that are organized centrally and are integral to the children's learning experiences;
- windows, and dividing walls made of glass, that reinforce a continuous connection between outside and inside;
- an *atelier*, or creative workshop, imaginatively resourced, where children work with an *atelierista* (an artist who is a part of the staff team);
- mini-*ateliers* – well-resourced art workshops attached to classrooms;
- flexible divisions of classroom space that include private spaces for children;
- furniture that has a variety of imaginative as well as practical uses;

- resources that are plentiful, well-organized and accessible;
- improvised materials that provide important stimuli for children's inventive representations and ongoing topics.

The child

Distinctive aspects of the Reggio Emilia approach include children being given opportunity to:

- seek out relationships in small groups, negotiate and plan with peers and adults, and share their personal objects and stories from home;
- use narrative extensively and rely on stories that project them into imaginary worlds;
- have responsibility for controlling powerful and imaginative use of light sources;
- use materials and spaces in a variety of complex, creative and imaginative ways;
- prepare for meals and rest times with little help from adults, and take their rest on bed rolls, in an area of the classroom that is remote and often dimly lit;
- work in the *piazza* (central area) as a part of small very tolerant groups who manage themselves effectively.

With the Reggio Emilia approach there is a reaffirmation of the importance of the decisions that children are able to make. Abbott and Nutbrown (2001: 5) identify characteristics of the approach that are easily transferable to work in schools with older children. They are identified as:

1 The ability that the teachers have to *listen* to children and by so doing gain real insight into their understanding.
2 *Time* given to discussion of projects where children participate.
3 *Time* given to aspects of the curriculum that allow teachers to stay 'connected' in their thinking with children and their families.
4 *Time* given to revisiting work done previously, allowing children to discuss and reflect on their development.
5 *Cooperation* and a cooperative way of working.
6 *Educatori* or teachers who work in pairs and share the teaching and organization of a group of children.

Teachers remain with the same group of children for three years. This is an aspect of the approach that is unfamiliar to the majority of schools in England. Edwards *et al.* (1998) see the interpretation of this educational approach as a sharing of culture and an understanding of the relationship and the dichotomy between the needs of individual children and collaboration with the community.

The children in the Reggio Emilia schools are characterized by their self-assurance, natural curiosity, high levels of involvement and sensitive interaction with one another. They ask for adult advice and are eager to share the development of their work. The work shows individuality, evidence of high-quality problem solving and sophisticated representational skills. The children's response to adult visitors is relaxed and very accommodating in spite of language barriers.

An inclusive approach

Polly has a class of 8- and 9-year-old children (Cameo 2). Her approach is influenced by the school's inclusive policy where all children are valued as individuals and children with special educational needs have places in all classrooms. The school behaviour policy suggests that respect between teachers and children is arrived at with children being encouraged to share decision making with the adults, with an emphasis on belonging and participating rather than on external control (Coulby 1995).

The teacher

The environment is organized to allow children space to pursue their own interests. An area with a comfortable settee invites relaxation. Children are free to use this area when tasks have been completed. In this environment work is valued. There is no extraneous clutter and children have space to move naturally and to interact freely. There is no hint of patronization or sarcasm in Polly's interchange with the children. Polly moves the lesson on quickly and confidently. Number bonds to 20 are explored in a systematic, creative and skilfully differentiated way. The children are encouraged to self-select their need to work with Polly by identifying their weakness and the need to go through the process

Figure 5.1   An area with a comfortable settee invites relaxation

again. Fisher (1995) discusses ways to create effective communities for learning and suggests that an independent learning environment should develop a climate in which the community is important and respect for the group engenders trust, support and communication. Polly ensures that children are aware of their own needs and understand how to identify them. She also encourages children to be aware of the needs of others. Fisher (1996) sees the need for the teacher to place the child in a negotiating position where there can be increased autonomy and understanding of the purpose of learning. Polly has adopted this strategy as a part of her classroom ethos and established a partnership between her and the children.

Polly sets the scene for the day by:

- allowing children to read or talk freely. She respects individual requests and demonstrates that systems are in place for each child to have responsibility on a rota basis;
- using a quiet introduction, with a German greeting, that engages the children's interest;
- approaching the 'housekeeping', or everyday classroom rituals, in a systematic and engaging manner with effective use of eye contact;
- showing sincerity and an interest in children's contributions.

In the cameo we also see Polly:

- using a manner that encourages children to approach her with their problems;
- gaining respect for her authority but able to engage easily with the children through the use of tentative responses to their questions;
- allowing children to assume ownership of particular topics;
- taking time to listen to children.

During the lesson she treats children fairly and is very aware of the individual progress that they are making. She understands the need to differentiate their tasks. She is alert to particular needs, firm about the boundaries, and ensures that questions and ideas are followed through. Polly uses impressive strategies to help children to avoid failure. The structure of the lesson moves quite subtly from whole-class teaching to smaller, differentiated group teaching and individual support. The behaviour policy in place in the school allows children to express feelings and encourages responsibility for individual behaviour. The positive approach requires children to share decision making with adults, and the emphasis is on belonging and participation, rather than on external control. Polly is aware of each child during the lesson and gives individual reward 'points' from time to time. Brief mentions are made of 'golden time' or free time given on Friday afternoons as a reward for group success during the week.

No policy or set of ambitious statements can work without effective interaction between the teacher and the children. Teachers with an understanding of the issues related to 'self' are likely to help children to become more independent in their attempts to make sense of new problems. Merry (1998) discusses *off task* children as posing a possible threat to some teachers, by indicating that they are receiving incompetent teaching. These children may be bored, or being given work that lacks challenge or is too difficult. Polly's strategies are, however, very clear. She is able to:

- hide any frustration that she feels about children who have not grasped the concepts of number bonds to 20 and similarly those to whom the 'inverse process' is still a mystery;
- challenge children's ideas to further their learning;
- be aware of those children who are 'off task' and monitor them closely.

Polly allows children to take responsibility for the process, the pace and the outcome of their learning. Apart from the initial discussion, her focus is not only on 'teaching', but also on the underrated concept of 'the facilitation of learning' (Rogers 1983). We are often quick to dismiss the ideas of previous decades and to be distracted by new approaches to teaching and learning. We neglect 'the conditions that encourage self-initiated, significant, experiential and gut-level learning by the whole person' (Rogers 1983: 121). Sylva (1997) indicates ways to avoid a reinvention of the wheel. Nothing is new, but reinventing ideas rather than incorporating them into a foundation for learning is counterproductive. Polly, as a teacher, has the responsibility for setting targets with children and ensuring that they have the opportunity to achieve prescribed goals. Her own targets are:

- to offer the children knowledge about number bonds to 20 and the strategies of the 'inverse process';
- to maintain children's self-esteem and positive self-attitude in her diverse class group;
- to establish the relationship between self-esteem and success;
- to maintain an understanding of the need for differentiation and the importance of the process as well as the outcome.

The children in Polly's class use many quick-fire responses to problems, as a part of their daily programme, and provide a range of correct and incorrect answers. They respect each other's responses and there is no laughter, hand waving or other negative signals from the children. Polly uses all the replies to scaffold learning, occasionally praising children and never ridiculing them. The children respond confidently. They know that the environment is a safe one in which to try out their ideas, and one in which the skilfully differentiated follow-up work will help to clarify misconceptions. The differing abilities of these children is apparent but is not made overt. The whole-school approach to behaviour management is very carefully documented and has had an important influence on Polly's approach with the children.

Rogers (1983) writes about significant learning being dependent on personal relationships between facilitators and learners. In a climate where teaching and the skills of teachers are constantly under review, it is important to recall the educational experiences during the 1960s to 1980s and to ask whether we should be building on the positive views of children's development and education dominant in many schools during that period. Whatever the political climate, effective education stems from a respect for children and an understanding of their development. This message should always be at the heart of the education system.

The child

I had informal discussions with the children in Polly's class over a period of several weeks. Conversation covered a wide range of issues, with questions relating to space, resources, organization and interaction in the environment. My intention was to find out how much the children felt involved with their classroom and outdoor space, the level of independence they were given and how the environment affected their motivation. From observation, the children appeared to be comfortable and very confident in a variety of personal and collaborative roles. Key points that arose illustrate the ethos within which Polly operates.

1 The children have a clear idea of personal responsibility and the responsibility that they have for others. They discussed the use of the playground and the system of taking turns to play with younger children.
2 The children understand their rights and the procedure they need to follow if they feel they have been wronged.
3 They feel that their classroom is a friendly place and that they can make suggestions, organize their own materials and work independently.
4 The children recognize that Polly listens to children's points of view and tells them very clearly when they need to think about their actions.
5 Polly is very pleased to hear about children's interests outside school and is always sharing particular incidents with the whole class.
6 Polly shares aspects of her own life with the children. 'She's funny. All the teachers in this school are like real people.'

The High/Scope approach

The High/Scope curriculum provides an active learning approach that focuses on cognitive orientation. One of the premises is that through interacting with objects, ideas, people and events children construct new knowledge. Hohmann *et al.* (1995) describe the approach as providing developmentally appropriate, active experiences for children, with opportunities for intellectual development through:

- direct action on objects;
- reflection on actions;
- development of intrinsic motivation, invention and generativity;
- problem solving.

The programme was developed in response to the failure of high school students from the poorest neighbourhoods of Ypsilanti in Michigan. A curriculum was designed to serve young children who were deemed to be 'at risk'. The first project in 1962 was known as the Perry Preschool Project. The second project, the Preschool Curriculum Demonstration Project, was designed to compare the effectiveness of the Cognitively Oriented Curriculum (the High/Scope approach), the Language Training Curriculum (a didactic curriculum model) and the Unit-based Curriculum (traditional nursery school model). This project was to become a longitudinal study with research findings showing that young adults who had experienced the High/Scope approach were found to be better adjusted socially, more likely to be home owners, less likely to have stayed in the same class for a second year and less likely to have been in jail. A study that replicated the High/Scope research took place in Portugal (Nabuco and Sylva 1995). In this project three distinct approaches to teaching and learning were studied: the High/Scope approach, the Formal Skills approach (didactic approach) and the Nursery School programme (a more traditional approach). The High/Scope programme provided a balanced approach to the curriculum with the Formal Skills approach allowing children no choice and the Nursery School programme giving unlimited choice.

The results of the Portuguese study were in agreement with those of Schweinhart and Weikart (1997). Sylva and Nabuco (1996) demonstrated that children attending the High/Scope programme had improved outcomes in reading, writing and self-esteem, and a lower anxiety level than their counterparts in formal skills settings and traditional nursery settings.

Significant features of the High/Scope programme discussed by Hohmann *et al.* (1995) include:

Figure 5.2 Cleaning the table after 'work-time'!

- home visits where teachers help parents to understand the school perspective on children's development and learning;
- parents introducing teachers to the variety of interests and needs of their children;
- a structured daily routine: circle time, planning time, work time, clean-up time, review time, small-group time and outside time (Brown 1990);
- space organized into work areas, and collated accessible resources and materials;
- an independent approach to planning, working and reviewing;
- a set of *key experiences* that cover personal and social development, affective development and cognitive development.

The child

One of the benefits of the High/Scope approach is the 'shaping of children's autonomy, decision making and feelings of control' (Schweinhart and Weikart 1997: 93). There has been speculation, as well as research evidence, that feeling in control of one's life has positive benefits for future social commitment. Schweinhart and Weikart (1997: 93) suggest that classroom environments have a profound influence 'in shaping children's autonomy, decision making and feelings of control'. Various interpretations of this framework have had significant influence on primary education in England. The very young children in Karen's early years unit (Cameo 3) are not only confident in sorting out the continuity of their working programme, but are able to reflect on the work of another child. They are able to accept Karen's sensitive intervention. The daily programme is carried out in a happy working environment where the expectation is that children manage their day-to-day activities independently and seek advice and help when it will move their thinking forward. The High/Scope curriculum has changed significantly over the last 25 years. It has moved from a pure Piagetian approach with experiences planned for children to acquire classification, seriation and representation to one where planning now involves the development of social skills and social cohesion (Sylva 1998).

Conclusion

In this chapter, views on an independent approach to teaching and learning have been taken from three separate starting points. There are inevitable similarities between these views. Two clear strands run through each approach. These are the careful structuring of the educational climate and the level of trust and responsibility given to children. There are many thoughtful and challenging approaches to teaching and learning already in primary classrooms. Alongside these there is also uncertainty, among some teachers, about how best to balance the developmental needs of children with the need to achieve the curriculum requirements. The educational frameworks introduced in this chapter are based on sound intellectual principles but are evolving and changing in line with the changing needs of societies. The centrality of the child is the focus of each approach. The child's contribution to the community and the positive interaction between adults and children are also considerable strengths. Also apparent, in each approach, is the value placed on what is familiar, what interests children and what they already know. Merry (1998) recognizes 'that social factors are often not made explicit', but they have an important effect on the climate for learning. Merry sees children as being influenced by the macro context of the culture outside the classroom as well as the micro context of the classroom. The effect, on children, of these varying contexts seriously influences their ability to be independent. Responses from the survey teachers frequently showed little regard for any influences on children outside school and consequently children's wider knowledge, skills and understanding often went unnoticed.

Questions

1 Do you review the strategies that you use to help children to develop independence?
2 Where do you look for inspiration to complement, change or extend the practice in your classroom?
3 Could children help to organize a more independent classroom ethos?

6

Bringing the outside inside: independence and the topic approach to learning

Cameo 1

A class of 10-year-old children is following a short topic on India. The theme had started, during the previous week, with celebrations for the festival of Diwali. These had been followed by discussion of the possible similarities and probable differences between the children's village and a village in the desert region of northern India. The outcomes of the topic have not been fully defined, although curricular requirements for geography, design and technology, and art have been considered. Hilary, a guest speaker who travels in India, has been invited to talk to the children. She starts by asking them what they already know about India. They volunteer ideas about food, clothing, homes, animals and decoration. The children seem inspired and are eager to share their experiences. The practical work starts with an investigation of a wide-ranging collection of everyday and ceremonial Indian textiles.

Cameo 2

A class of 10- and 11-year-olds is following a topic on the environment. They had been introduced to the structural and ephemeral approach to art, used by the artist Andy Goldsworthy. The children are visiting a university campus, where the parkland environment is rich in natural detritus. They work in the grounds for several hours, creating sculptures and structures with natural materials. Their 'assemblages' are then left to return to nature. The children take photographs to provide an ongoing record of their work.

They evaluate the work *in situ*, share their ideas and compare photographs. They are to follow up this experience and adapt the techniques and the process in their inner city school environment.

Introduction

Relevant and challenging project work gives opportunities for children to work both collaboratively and independently. The cameos illustrate themes that draw on and extend children's first-hand experience. The learning objectives for each topic are related to particular curriculum areas. The true potential of successful projects may, however, not be fully realized until the process as well as the outcomes are evaluated. 'Bringing the outside inside' suggests the importance of children making contributions to topics and extending their personal frames of reference. In each case the topics have been enriched by excursions or by listening to an expert.

The teacher

Teachers individually and collectively have to reappraise their teaching in response to the changing needs of their pupils and the impact of economic, social and cultural change.
(DfEE/QCA 1999: 13)

The move to a subject-based curriculum has tended to fragment or create unnatural divisions of knowledge. Any strategy that serves to centralize understanding and allow teachers and children to look at knowledge that can be shared will stimulate interest and encourage enthusiastic, independent learning. 'Scaffolding' learning stems from the work of Vygotsky and Bruner. Scaffolding refers to the wide range of activities through which the adult or the more expert peer assists the learner to achieve goals, which would otherwise be beyond him or her. Scaffolding is a flexible and child-centred supportive strategy. As the child masters new skills the adult is able gradually to remove the scaffolding. Within each of the themes illustrated in the cameos there is no didactic teaching. The children are able to draw on their skills and previous experience and respond to the stimulus in a positive and creative way. It is important to recognize that the classroom climate should encourage '... the socio-cultural and discursive bases of knowledge and learning' (Edwards and Mercer 1987: 168).

Webb and Vulliamy (1996) write about the unprecedented planning demands placed on teachers. Suschitzky and Chapman (1998) discuss the effect that the Education Reform Act and Ofsted requirements have had on teachers' control over the classroom climate. They comment on the tendency for conformity in the curriculum content and methodology. This tendency has been compounded further with uncertainties in curriculum organization, following the introduction of the literacy and numeracy strategies (DfEE 1998; DfEE 1999). Teachers have to operate within a framework of whole-school policies and schemes of work but there should still be some choice of curriculum content where learning experiences are sensitively and flexibly constructed.

In spite of external pressure the choices that many teachers make about curriculum selection and presentation are still shaped by personal beliefs and values. These values have been developed through cultural experience and the chances that teachers have taken to reflect on and evaluate the effectiveness of their practice. Woods and Jeffrey (1996: 1), when considering the significance of creative teaching, found that teachers had initially viewed the National Curriculum as a challenge to their powers of 'coping and appropriating'. They discuss how teachers found ways of negotiating a route through the seemingly opposing issues of 'creativity or control' and of exercising their own professional judgement about the efficacy of different models of curriculum delivery. Inevitably, as Pollard (1997: 192) suggests, particular values held by the teacher which she or he incorporates into the curriculum are seen as 'legitimate objects of learning' by the children. School values are made clear to children through the books, resources and IT programmes selected, as well as visits and the general classroom climate. Children soon understand whether or not value is placed on their prior experience and understanding.

Topics, themes and projects

Webb and Vulliamy (1996) see topic work as a method of organizing learning that involves enquiry. It can be used to deliver material in separate subjects or as themes, in which a number of subjects are integrated. What is meant by a topic is open to interpretation. Katz and Chard (1990: 2) prefer the term 'project' and add 'topic', 'theme' and 'unit' as variables. They describe a 'project' as 'an in-depth study of a particular topic that one or more children undertake'. Examples in this chapter show project/ topic approaches that encourage high-energy involvement by children. There are illustrations of interaction between teachers, children and the wider community and of the value placed on children's spontaneous as well as their researched responses. HMI reports in the 1990s described topic work as undemanding, aimless, superficial and lacking in progression (Webb and Vuillamy 1996). Ironically, Katz and Chard (1990) describe practice related to the requirements of our current curriculum requirements as mindless and time wasting for children.

The Reggio Emilia experience (Chapter 5) places importance on a thematic approach to teaching and learning. Children are given time to work through problems, follow interests and to research and develop conceptual understanding. They communicate in a variety of ways using what Malaguzzi calls their 'hundred languages' (Edwards *et al.* 1998: 3). If these very young children are given the chance to research and solve problems to a high level, it is surely possible for older children to take part in experiences that will give them the tools to operate effectively across a range of situations.

If we take a serious view of helping children to experience joy in a commitment to learning, account must be taken of children's wider knowledge and experience and of their existing competence and independence. Learning is often expected to take place in an environment that is unfamiliar and possibly irrelevant to many pupils. Objectives and outcomes are largely defined in advance and progress towards them is rigorously monitored. The requirement for collecting specific *evidence* for assessment of children's progress towards the curriculum goals often prevents them from taking a more exploratory approach to learning. As a consequence of the mechanization of the educational process, topic-based learning is now less used across the primary age phase. The emphasis on delivery of discrete subjects, particularly with older children, has led to many teachers losing confidence in 'bringing the outside inside' and considering the holistic nature of learning.

Topic work, although appealing to some teachers, raises doubts in the minds of others. Evidence from observation and discussion with the survey teachers shows that doubt about using a thematic approach probably stems from the uncertain nature of objectives and the unpredictable and possibly ephemeral nature of the outcomes. Many teachers feel under pressure to *prove* that learning is taking place and feel that a topic approach would leave them with outcomes that are hard to evaluate or to relate to specific curriculum goals. A topic approach also causes some teachers to be uncertain of exposing themselves to the uncertainties of a way of working in which children behave independently and are given responsibility.

The child

A thematic approach to the curriculum is still a valued part of children's experience in some schools. Creative teachers will always see possibilities for capitalizing on children's intrinsic motivation and the way their interest can be sparked by varied approaches to the curriculum (Katz and Chard 1990). Duffy (1998) writes of creative early years teachers needing to know children well and to support them by introducing information and skills at the point at which they are needed. Duffy's recommendations have relevance for older children as well. Children in Key Stage 2 will have had more experience both in and out of school. They will have developed skills and concepts that transfer easily across subject areas. These children need the chance to take part in topics and to contribute additional knowledge, skills and understanding from their wider experiences. Many children are more comfortable with computers than their teachers. They should be encouraged to share their knowledge for the benefit of both adults and other children. There are many more areas where children's knowledge is extensive and it is this knowledge that can be tapped into through the many facets and opportunities that are offered by a thematic or topic approach.

The context

The two cameos at the start of the chapter indicate opportunities for learning in which children can work at their own pace and share their interest and expertise. Criteria for providing an effective framework for topics will include:

- choice of theme that has relevance to the children, whether it is based on something familiar or something exotic;
- clear objectives for satisfying the requirements of a range of curriculum areas;
- opportunities for complementing and extending children's prior and current knowledge and skills;
- flexibility over the direction taken by the project, to allow for unforeseen and spontaneous developments;
- continuous dialogue between adults and children to monitor enthusiasm and evaluate learning;
- chances to recap and revisit ideas in order to consolidate what has been learned so far and to help children to find ways of moving forward;
- opportunities for children to develop personal, social, creative and affective skills;
- opportunities for assessment in traditional and non-traditional ways.

In Cameo 1 the children had had prior introduction to India through the traditional festival of Diwali. Hilary, the guest speaker, uses a sensitive approach with the children. Her thoughtful questions allow them to share their personal knowledge of Indian food, clothing, textiles and stories of relatives who had travelled in India. She shares her personal experiences through slides, artefacts, textiles, photographs and books. In less than an hour the topic comes to life and the children are interested because what had seemed to be 'exotic' was being made familiar by referring to their existing knowledge. The topic is short but the children have the chance to work at their own pace and follow particular interests within its framework. The approach satisfies the requirements suggested for reviewing a school policy on topic work (Webb and Vuillamy 1996: 59). Table 6.1 shows evidence of the organization and extension of these requirements.

Topic 1

An Indian village

Hilary, the visiting 'expert', draws on the children's first-hand experience by allowing them to share aspects of Indian culture and tradition that have already influenced their own lives. The ideas generated confirm the view that an initial focus on children's existing knowledge gives the topic a secure starting point. Common knowledge is arrived at and illustrated by the following list of ideas.

Food: 'It's hot!' 'No, not hot, it's spicy hot'. 'I like Chinese, my dad likes Indian.' 'My mum makes Indian food.'

Textiles: Fabric used as decoration in one child's home – 'My mum bought some of that with the mirrors in the market.' 'There's a lady with a sari in our street.'

Elephants: 'They're big. My brother went to Thailand and he went on an elephant!'

Jewellery and decoration: 'They have patterns on their hands and red marks on their heads and rings in their noses.' 'My sister has three rings in her ears and one in her belly button.'

Incense sticks: 'They smell strong. I have them in my bedroom sometimes.'

Hilary introduces the children to a magical mystery tour of her own experiences of rural India. Using slides and overhead transparencies, a stimulating display of textiles and artefacts, music, photographs and dialogue, she is able to transmit something of the faiths, lifestyle, climate, architecture, fabric design, crafts, animals, community life and food of India. Her time with the children is short, but the buzz of excitement is noticeable and the engagement with a variety of stimuli allows them to empathize with the ideas that are generated. After Hilary's visit the class teacher was sensitive to the relevance that the Indian topic needed to have for the children and chose to extend their thinking along the lines of their original 'brainstorm'. Thus fabric decoration and clothing, food, elephants, and aspects of art and transport were chosen to extend the knowledge of Indian culture and tradition.

The Indian topic was a lively and very valuable project. It complemented the rest of the curriculum, drew on children's prior knowledge, encouraged enquiry and gave a solid purpose to skills that were easily transferred to new tasks (see Table 6.1). The children had an element of choice in the directions that they took, and specific as well as intermittent time to achieve their outcomes. The quality of their work and the pride that they took in completing the tasks reflected individual and collective achievement. The skill in maintaining motivation and intellectual engagement lay in the teacher's ability to provide ongoing

Figure 6.1 An elephant inspired by the decorative Indian textile tradition
Samantha, aged 10 years

academic and practical instruction as the need arose. The teacher accepted that, unlike the preplanned part of the curriculum, the topic allowed emergence of different directions and involved negotiation and independent choice. The topic led to the development of a framework for considering the similarities and differences between the children's local village and an Indian village.

Topic 2

Andy Goldsworthy

In Cameo 2, the visit to the university campus is the highlight of a very successful and wide-ranging project on the environment. The children had spent three weeks working in their local, urban area, considering its architecture, facilities, traffic problems, pollution and litter. Prior to their visit the children learned something of the artwork of Andy Goldsworthy. A video discussing his assemblages had allowed them to understand his union with nature and his need to create in the natural environment. They were very interested in books and displays of photographs of

Table 6.1 Overview of Indian village project

A village in northern India	
Aims	*Evaluation*
To introduce the Indian subcontinent To consider aspects of life in a village in Rajasthan and to provide tools for comparison and contrast with aspects of life in an English village **Learning objectives** • to be able to use maps and secondary sources; • to gain knowledge of life in rural India; • to make a link between the topic and elements of geography, design and technology and art.	The staff had agreed upon the aims, intentions and purposes of topic teaching. The topic approach was used regularly as a vehicle for teaching and learning.
Topic development Teacher introduces the geographical elements of the topic and celebrates Divali with the children. Guest speaker elicits children's ideas on India and their experiences of Indian influences on their lives. Contributions made by children and families throughout the topic – artefacts, recipes, textiles, and photographs.	Monitoring of children's initial ideas and how they affect the direction and content of the topic. Resources and ideas include verbal evidence of prior knowledge, first-hand experience, secondary sources (books, photographs, video).
Curriculum elements considered: **art** (painting and relationship of Indian painting to the work of the book illustrator, Jane Ray); **design and technology** (fabric design, cookery and puppet making);	Consideration was given to the balance of subject elements in the topics over the year, as well as concepts, skills and language that needed to be taught for the curriculum areas linked for this topic.

Table 6.1   (Cont'd)

A village in northern India	
Aims	*Evaluation*
fabric design and the cultural influence of textile design and use is a natural extension of children's previous knowledge of creating patterns using a variety of techniques	Evidence of children's work, discussion with the children and observation of their general inventive and creative use of resources to replicate Indian textile design.
geography – consideration of the location of India and the climate, agriculture and rural lifestyle of a village in northern India – the children had previously studied their local environment, which was also rural.	The rural area of Rajasthan in India provided a useful comparison and extension to subject knowledge for previous work with a local village in England.

	Reflection and assessment
The topic proved to be very popular and progress was shared verbally and visually at any available moment.	Progression within and between particular subjects was monitored and mapped against the requirements of the National Curriculum.
Outcome – display of textile designs; sketch books, interactive puppet performance and Indian meal provided a culmination of the contributions from the whole class as well as their parents.	Individual progress was charted through assessment of particular physical and human aspects of geography
	• comparisons between Indian village life and life in their own village;
	• use of maps;
	• evidence from sketch/design books;
	• observation and record keeping by the teacher.
	Although the outcome included integration of the three curriculum areas, clear progress in each was monitored.

his sculptures. Goldsworthy (1990: introduction) says, 'For me, looking, touching, material, place and form are all inseparable from the resulting work. It is difficult to say where one stops and another begins.' Using Goldsworthy's style appealed to the children, as did the freedom that they were given to choose their work location, select a range of natural material and create sculptures in small groups. Goldsworthy's work grows, stays and decays, and this was the first time that the children had really understood that the process and the outcome were of equal importance but that the finished work would return to nature. From their short experience of working in this way the children gained:

- an awareness of natural objects and the space around them;
- some understanding of form, shape, texture, flexibility and the possibilities afforded by the natural world;
- some experience of Goldsworthy's recognition of change in the weather as their work had started in sunlight and continued in light rain;
- an understanding of the characteristics of the materials that they were using and of their possibilities for creating shapes and form;
- knowledge of using digital cameras to keep a lasting record of work at what Goldsworthy calls 'its height';
- introduction to art work that is left in situ, ephemeral and allowed to decay;
- an overall sensitivity to their surroundings and their role as visitors;
- a sense of responsibility for the environment by having the opportunity to work without causing damage.

The use of digital cameras ensured that the children had a means by which they could assess their work. The use of photographic evidence also allowed them to record their work in the same way as Goldsworthy. Thus the children had a photographic record and the 'artwork' was left to return to nature. The children worked in small groups and showed a high degree of cooperation and negotiation. Ideas were accepted and rejected as more appropriate solutions were arrived at. There was an air of excitement and enthusiastic response as the work progressed. The children had obvious pride in the outcomes.

Figures 6.2 and 6.3 A photographic record of artwork then left to return to nature

Why use the topic approach?

The topic approach has more to offer than simple satisfaction of single subject requirements. If teachers have the confidence to 'bring the outside inside' they will reap the benefit of collective knowledge and the inspiration of unforeseen directions.

Katz and Chard (1990: 4) describe the academic curriculum as oriented to specific goals and providing a *vertical* approach that moves the learner to the next stage. They see the project approach as a *horizontal* approach, or one 'that equips the learner to solve current problems within and outside the classroom'. It is a way of deepening children's understanding of their experiences in the wider environment. With younger children this premise is still largely undisputed, but the project approach with older children could still make an important contribution to the encouragement of wider intellectual engagement, creative connections and inspiration. There should be a time in school when narrow curriculum opportunities can be relaxed and where opportunities for genuine, ongoing work can take place. In the previous section a set of criteria for providing an effective framework for a topic approach was suggested. The list below complements those criteria and considers the value of a topic approach for broadening the scope of curriculum provision.

A topic approach allows teachers to:

- use independent and collaborative approaches to planning and organization that complement the initial ideas for the topic whilst valuing and incorporating children's contributions;
- have some clear curriculum connections and learning goals as well as tentative aspirations that leave room for surprises;
- be innovative and creative in their interpretation of themes;
- give children a sense of ownership and independence;
- have opportunities for whole-class teaching, group work and individual work whenever each teaching style is seen to be appropriate;
- reconsider teaching and learning strategies in the light of what they observe about children during the project;
- provide a variety of stimuli to help children to find relevance in the subject matter;
- allow children time to proceed independently, through genuine research that may follow personal interests.

The child

The Reggio Emilia philosophy (Chapter 5) recognizes that topics for study may come from children themselves, from subjects that have naturally engaged and interested children previously, or from the family and the wider community (Valentine 1999). The possible outcomes of a topic may be anticipated and provided for in advance. Predictions may be made as to possible directions. On the other hand, the topic may not have a defined direction and the lead will be taken from the children's responses. An expert infrastructure is always in place to support and extend ideas. This approach highlights an understanding of intrinsic motivation and of children's prior understanding. Room is always left for the knowledge, inspiration and creativity of the children. Suschitzky and Chapman (1998) echo this approach when they say that if use is made of the wider environment for learning then children will experience the school learning environment in the light of their cultural background. They will then appreciate the extension of these experiences, with skilful support from teachers, in their further development.

For topic work to be an effective springboard for children's learning there has to be a sincere approach from teachers and parents as well as the children themselves. Children's and teachers' prior knowledge should be utilized, tentative learning objectives formulated, rigid outcomes avoided and varied and creative ways found for assessment. The approach to successful topics has to be one of genuine enquiry with related tasks and research helping children to extend their knowledge and understanding of the world.

A topic approach should allow children to:

- integrate relevant areas of knowledge with increasing independence and motivation;
- demonstrate existing skills and knowledge and extend their experiences in collaboration with their peers;
- make connections between what is familiar and what is seemingly 'exotic';
- move from their first-hand experience of the world to a view of the world presented through secondary sources (books, photographs, videos, ICT);
- understand that their primary engagement with ideas has relevance for the ideas that will develop from a range of additional first-hand and abstract experiences.

Context

The Reggio Emilia approach to teaching and learning (Katz and Cesarone 1994; Hendrick 1997; Edwards *et al*. 1998; Valentine 1999) does not establish the curriculum in advance. It ensures that:

- projects can provide a framework for holistic learning for children and teachers;
- teachers identify general goals and hypothesize about the directions that projects might take;
- projects may be decided by the children or they may be based on themes that have interested previous groups of children;
- children are monitored closely and encouraged to discuss the development of projects.

The topic approach and older children

The approach used in the Reggio Emilia schools is used with children from 0 to 6 years of age. The underlying philosophy and practice is rooted in experiential learning, dialogue with children and value placed on shared understanding between children and adults (Chapter 5). These values support effective topic work and suggest that a topic approach for children across the primary age phase is an efficient way of incorporating children's prior experience and developing understanding. As has been said previously, although the framework for a topic may be planned in advance, effectiveness will be increased if children's knowledge, skills and understanding are monitored. The value of the topic will be further increased when children's views are sought and where there is encouragement for contributions from children. I am in full agreement with Alexander and Pollard who argue that an effective approach to the curriculum can still developed through projects in spite of criticism of the 'topics-based approach' (Alexander *et al*. 1992; Pollard 1997). The motivation and concentration shown by children engaged in this learning process and the ability of the children to express their knowledge can be achieved through what Malaguzzi called the 'hundred languages' or the many ways children find to express their ideas and to make creative connections (Valentine 1999).

How should the themes or topics be organized?

The teacher

The effect on some schools of the Plowden Committee's recommendations (CACE 1967) was to 'sustain practice which in visual terms might look attractive and busy but which lacked any serious educational rationale' (Alexander *et al.* 1992: 9). Alexander's report was based on reviews of previous evidence and current research into practice in schools. The report was written at a time when schools were going through significant change following the Education Reform Act. The report introduced the debate concerning subject delivery and topic delivery. Subject divisions had been seen as being 'inconsistent with the child's view of the world' (Alexander *et al.* 1992: 21), and introduction to the whole curriculum was thought of as helping children to construct meaning. Alexander *et al.* (1992: 27) contest these ideas by asserting that 'the integrity of the curriculum as a whole is hardly likely to be achieved by sacrificing the integrity of its constituent parts'. It is acknowledged, however, that topic work that focused on limited targets can contribute to learning. A distinction can be made between topics that involve:

- 'integration', which brings subjects together but allows the subjects to retain their identities;
- 'non-differentiation', which does not allow for separate subject identity.

Teachers of younger children were seen as favouring the non-differentiation viewpoint. The report acknowledges that teachers need to evaluate the strengths and weaknesses of approaches and to consider the suitability of whole-class teaching, group work and individual work for achieving different educational outcomes. Where does this leave the teacher and topic work?

Pollard (1997) recognizes that many teachers find a way through the apparent dichotomy between creative approaches and controlled responses. Topic work is alive and well in many schools, but there is the feeling of guilt, among some teachers, that causes them to relegate the topic to the end of the week or even the last week of term. Suschitzky and Chapman (1998) describe a dilemma faced by teachers who are trying to 'achieve an acceptable environment for learning'. They are described as hiding items of their personal philosophies in the cupboard and being angry, uncertain and confused as to how to proceed. There is, however, some resistance to unnecessary change and a return to an understanding of the need for appropriate experiences for young children in line with their development (Galton 1995).

One of the aims of this chapter has been to place the topic or thematic approach back on the agenda and to allow it to become an integrated and challenging part of the learning experience for children. A topic approach will require some or all of the following:

- teachers who value creative and divergent ways of working;
- teachers who are prepared to bring knowledge gained from reading and observation to the organization of effective topics;
- topics relevant to children, which challenge and extend previous experience and encompass specific curriculum directions;
- traditional written planning that provides accountability and gives a general idea of the direction of a project, its aims, objectives and outcomes;
- opportunities for extended planning that incorporates innovative ideas, new opportunities and divergence of direction;
- inclusion of ideas and contributions that stem from children, parents and the wider community;
- knowledge and understanding of the curriculum areas that are to be integrated;
- direct teaching, group collaboration and individual, independent research;
- a work base that has :
  - generic materials and resources (paint, paper, clay, computers, a library);
  - resources that are specifically related to the topic (artefacts, books, IT programmes, photographs);
  - opportunities for display, evaluation and sharing of ideas as appropriate;
- commitment to bringing the topic alive, making it relevant to the children, encouraging their contributions and introducing personal experience;
- formative and summative assessment that involves children and provides feedback for them.

The child

Discussion with children and 'brainstorming' elicits what they already know and allows them not only to share ideas but to understand how creative connections can be made from apparently unlikely starting points. A lack of explicitness of purpose for teaching was criticized by Edwards and Mercer (1987: 169). They observed 'experiential learning', with children finding things out for themselves, but also observed teachers telling children why they were doing activities and where these activities fitted into what had gone before and what was still to come. It is the latter observation that shows teachers and children having 'shared a conceptual sense of the meaning and significance of experience and activity'. If children's experience is taken into account and their opinions sought then their learning will become more relevant.

In order to take children's ideas into account, strategies have to be put in place. 'Brainstorming' describes the democratic process of generating and accepting ideas for taking a topic forward. The process of 'brainstorming' has declined in popularity because our curriculum is often seen now to be already defined and explicit. In the past, 'brainstorming' as a starting point for topic work often failed to be effective for two reasons:

- spurious connections were made, to ensure that all subject areas were included in a project. McNamara (1994: 85) talks of the subject matter being taught as 'ad hoc and eclectic';
- predetermined outcomes were established for a topic regardless of the issues and interests raised during a 'brainstorming' session.

The Reggio Emilia approach to learning (Valentine 1999) allows teachers to have personal knowledge of children, to respect their ideas and to encourage them to reflect and to question. The curriculum is not one that is delivered to children but rather one that develops through close observation of children, extensive documentation and collection of evidence of children's learning. Children who are given the opportunity to take decisions, to hypothesize, to work collaboratively, to share ideas in a supportive environment, have the opportunity to be independent. This is a version of curriculum experience that should be modified and offered to all children, regardless of their age.

Teacher, child and the curriculum

An aim for project work is to allow children to widen their perspective of the world and to make intellectual links between what they already know and new information and creative possibilities. The project needs to be chosen carefully and negotiated between adults and children. The projects discussed in this chapter involved older children working independently and taking responsibility for aspects of the project's direction. At no time, with either project, did the teachers lose sight of the specific outcomes required for the curriculum. They had the skills to give children responsibility for their learning while at the same time having clear planning strategies, high expectations for effort and presentation, and flexibility and creativity in gathering ideas and resources. They were able to challenge children and present them with a variety of problems to solve. For example:

Teacher: You've seen the glorious range of textiles from India. Now study them carefully and find an element of design that appeals to you. How will you develop it to make your own design on fabric? Which techniques will you use?

Teacher: You watched the demonstration of puppet making. Can you collect your materials and work in twos? You will have to take it in turn to use the saws and the bench hooks. Please help each other and remember the health and safety rules.

Teacher: Can we all gather together and look at this structure? Helen and Zamion have joined grasses together, using one of Goldsworthy's techniques. Can you ask them how they did it? Move on to Jane's and Hannah's 'nest'. They have used a weaving technique. Go back to your own structures and look at the number of techniques you have used and how successful they have been.

A comment from one child after the conclusion of the project on India points to a successful ending: 'All we need to do now is to go to India.'

Conclusion

When teachers use an effective project or thematic approach they are encouraging children to share prior knowledge and to arrive at mutually acceptable frameworks (Bruner 1996). Teachers must be prepared to involve children and other adults in planning, be tentative about possible directions and prepared for unexpected outcomes. Schools are required to provide a framework for teaching and opportunities for learning that complement the requirements of the National Curriculum but this should not detract from giving children the broadest possible perspective on the world. Our current academic curriculum framework encourages an approach to learning that is separated into subjects with linear, measurable outcomes. However, within this framework there are opportunities for a more balanced and broader approach to teaching and learning. Progression in learning should be made through positive partnerships. The National Curriculum suggests that teachers must be given '. . . discretion to find the best ways to inspire in their pupils a joy and commitment to learning that will last a lifetime' (DfEE/QCA 1999: 1).

7

Conclusion: the end of the journey

The journey that started out to explore the reality of an independent approach to teaching and learning has ended. There has been open discussion, observation and analysis leading to a growing realization that independence in children's lives is important for what Laevers (2000) calls children's deep-level learning and emotional health.

I chose to explore independence through the use of cameos from both home and school. In this way, short stories about particular children were told. The story that concludes the journey concerns a universal child. The universal child represents children across the world, who have the right to receive respect for ideas and for developing dispositions and skills to manage their lives. This child, like all children, will have emotional, social and cultural attachments beyond the context of the school. S/he will bring these existing influences on his or her life to the educational situation, where teaching and learning should continuously accommodate his or her needs.

Education will increase the child's knowledge. The child will accommodate this knowledge and combine newly acquired skills and attitudes with a developing understanding of the world. Social competence and self-esteem will develop if the school climate is right and the child will apply what s/he learns to suit the life situation, which s/he hopes to influence. If the school supports the child's curiosity and drive to explore, s/he will be helped to gain confidence in communication and self-organization. S/he will be sensitive to the needs of others through the development of feelings and emotions. There will be opportunities for the child to stand back and reflect, affirm and rethink. S/he will learn to question his/her motives and intentions and to recognize his/her limitations and strengths.

The universally independent child will have worked at self-discipline and found creative solutions to problems. This child is developing a positive attitude to life and living, and is increasingly aware of how to manage his/her life and how to empathize with others. S/he knows how to use resources effectively and how best to contribute to his/her life at home and at school. This child is a strong communicator who has a sense of well-being and involvement in his/her learning. Undoubtedly if his/her creative expression can be combined with organizational skills, s/he has the ingredients for entrepreneurship.

Ensuring that children experience independence and have their individuality and vision valued poses a challenge to teachers. The journey of discovery, through the chapters of this book, has shown us that there are definitely two extremes along the independence continuum. In some settings there is an optimistic view of children's potential as managers and entrepreneurs. In others there is a tension between developmentally appropriate pedagogy and a didactic teaching style seen to be more expedient for achieving specific curriculum outcomes. These two extreme views are not mutually exclusive. Pedagogy that over-indulges individual needs should be tempered in the light of changing curriculum aims and the reality of expectations for large classes of children in the twenty-first century. On the other hand an over-restrictive approach to teaching and learning requires adaptation to give children the chance to make choices, organize themselves, and respond with energy and enthusiasm. The children of today are to be the adults of the future. As children and as adults they need the skills to make effective choices, to be courageous enough to stand up for what they believe in, to see things through and to know when to say 'no'!

A journey of this nature raises more questions than it answers. It is the question about autonomy (addressed in Chapter 1) that needs to be reconsidered. Doubt was raised about the nature and desirability of being autonomous. If autonomy means developing an inner strength and composure as well as gaining a better understanding of the human and the physical environment then autonomy must join independence and responsibility as dispositions with which children and teachers need to work. Opportunities for independence, responsibility and autonomy should be a reality for *all* children.

References

Abbott, L. and Nutbrown, C. (2001) *Experiencing Reggio Emilia*. Buckingham: Open University Press.

Alexander, R. (1995) *Versions of Primary Education*. London: Routledge.

Alexander, R. (2000) *Culture and Pedagogy*. Oxford: Blackwell.

Alexander, R., Rose, J., Woodhead, C. (1992) *Curriculum Organisation and Classroom Practice in Primary Schools*. London: HMSO.

Arnold, C. (2001) Sharing ideas with parents about key child development concepts, in M. Whalley, *Involving Parents in their Children's Learning*. London: Paul Chapman Publishing.

Athey, C. (1990) *Extending Thought in Young Children*. London: Paul Chapman Publishing.

Atkinson, S. (1992) *Mathematics with Reason*. London: Hodder and Stoughton.

Barrett, G. (1989) *Disaffection from School*. London: Falmer Press.

Bennett, N. (1976) *Teaching Styles and Pupil Progress*. London: Open Books.

Blenkin, G. and Kelly, V. (1992) *Assessment in Early Childhood Education*. London: Paul Chapman Publishing.

Blenkin, G. and Kelly, V. (2000) *The Concept of Infancy – A Case for Reconstruction*. In Early Years TACTYC International Journal of Research and Development. Stoke on Trent: Trentham.

Brown, G. and Wragg, G. (1993) *Questioning*. London: Routledge.

Brown, M. (1990) *The High/Scope Approach to the National Curriculum. 1: An Introduction*. Ypsilanti, MI: High/Scope Press.

Bruner, J.S. (1968) *Towards a Theory of Instruction*. New York, NY: W.W. Norton.

Bruner, J.S. (1996) *The Culture of Education*. Cambridge, MA: Harvard University Press.

CACE (Central Advisory Council for Education) (1967) *Children and Their Primary Schools* (Plowden Report). London: HMSO.

Caddell, D. (1998) *Numeracy Counts.* Dundee: Scottish Consultative Council on the Curriculum.

Calkins, L. (1986) *The Art of Teaching Writing.* Portsmouth, NH: Heinemann.

Ceppi, G., Zini, M. (eds) (1998) *Children, Spaces and Relations: Metaproject for an Environment for young Children.* Reggio Emilia: Reggio Children.

Chaplain, R. (2000) Helping children to persevere and be well motivated, in D. Whitebread (ed.) *The Psychology of Teaching and Learning in the Primary School.* London: Routledge/Falmer.

Collins, J., Insley, K. and Soler, J. (eds) (2001) *Developing Pedagogy, Researching Practice.* London: Paul Chapman Publishing.

Cook, D. and Finlayson, H. (1999) *Interactive Children, Communicative Teaching.* Buckingham: Open University Press.

Costello, P. (2000) *Thinking Skills and Early Childhood.* London: David Fulton.

Coulby, J. (1995) Behaviour Policy Number Twelve and Guidelines. Batheaston Church of England V.C. Primary School (unpublished).

Coulby, J. (1998) *Behaviour Policy and Guidelines.* Batheaston Church of England V.C. Primary School (unpublished).

Coulby, D. (2000) *Beyond the National Curriculum.* London: Routledge/Falmer.

Coulby, J. (2001) What do we mean by Inclusive Education? *Lecture to PGCE students Bath Spa University College,* 11 March.

Cullingford, C. (1990) *The Nature of Learning.* London: Cassell Educational Limited.

Czerniewska, P. (1992) *Learning about Writing.* Oxford: Blackwell.

Dahlberg, G., Moss, P. and Pence, A. (1999) *Beyond Quality in Early Childhood Education and Care.* London: Falmer Press.

De Boo (1999) *Enquiring Children, Challenging Teaching.* Buckingham: Open University Press.

DES (Department of Education and Science) (1985a) *Better Schools.* London: HMSO.

DES (Department of Education and Science) (1985b) *The Curriculum for 5–16.* London: HMSO.

DES (Department of Education and Science) (1990) *Starting with Quality: Report of the Committee of Inquiry into the Quality of Educational Experiences Offered to 3- and 4-year-olds* (Rumbold Report). London: HMSO.

DfEE (Department for Education and Employment) (1998) *The National Literacy Strategy.* London: HMSO.

DfEE (Department for Education and Employment) (1999) *The National Numeracy Strategy.* London: HMSO.

DfEE (Department for Education and Employment) (2000) *Research into Teacher Effectiveness. A Model of Teacher Effectiveness.* London: HMSO.

DfEE/QCA (Department for Education and Employment/Qualifications and Curriculum Authority) (1999) *The National Curriculum: Handbook for Primary Teachers*. London: DfEE and QCA.

DfEE/QCA (Department for Education and Employment/Qualifications and Curriculum Authority) (2000) *Curriculum Guidance for the Foundation Stage*. London: HMSO.

Donaldson, M. (1978) *Children's Minds*. Glasgow: Fontana.

Donaldson, M. (1992) *Human Minds: An Exploration*. London: Allen Lane.

Drummond, M.J. (1994) *Assessing Children's Learning*. London: Paul Chapman Publishing.

Duffy, B. (1998) *Supporting Creativity and Imagination in the Early Years*. Buckingham: Open University Press.

Edwards, C., Gandini, L. and Forman, G. (1998) *The Hundred Languages of Children*. London: Ablex Publishing Corporation.

Edwards, D. and Mercer, D. (1987) *Common Knowledge: The Development of Understanding in the Classroom*. London: Methuen.

Fisher, J. (1996) *Starting from the Child?* Buckingham: Open University Press.

Fisher, R. (1990) *Teaching Children to Think*. Cheltenham: Stanley Thornes.

Fisher, R. (1995) *Teaching Children to Learn*. Cheltenham: Stanley Thornes.

Furedi, F. (2001) *Paranoid Parenting*. London: Allen Lane, Penguin Press.

Galton, M. (1989) *Teaching in the Primary School*. London: David Fulton.

Galton, M. (1995) *Crisis in the Primary Classroom*. London: David Fulton.

Gardner, H. (1993) *Frames of Mind: The Theory of Multiple Intelligences*, 2nd edn. London: Fontana Press.

Goldsworthy, A. (1990) *Goldsworthy*. London: Viking.

Hall, N. (ed.) (1989) *Writing with Reason*. Sevenoaks: Hodder and Stoughton.

Hall, N. and Martello, J. (eds) (1996) *Listening to Children Think: Exploring Talk in the Early Years*. London: Hodder and Stoughton.

Hendrick, J. (1997) *First Steps toward Teaching the Reggio Way*. London: Prentice-Hall.

HMI (1985) *The Curriculum from 5 to 16. Curriculum Matters 2*. An HMI Series. London: HMSO.

Hohmann, M., Banet, B. and Weikart, D. (1995) *Young Children in Action*. Ypsilanti, MI: High/Scope Press.

Holt, J. (1965) *How Children Fail*. Harmondsworth: Penguin.

Hughes, M. (1986) *Children and Number*. Oxford: Blackwell.

Hurst, V. and Joseph, J. (1998) *Supporting Early Learning: The Way Forward*. Buckingham: Open University Press.

Johnston, J. (1996) *Early Explorations in Science*. Buckingham: Open University Press.

Katz, L. and Chard, S. (1990) *Engaging Children's Minds*. New Jersey, NJ: Ablex.

Kershner, R. (2000) Organising the physical environment of the classroom to support children's learning, in D. Whitebread (ed.) *The Psychology of Teaching and Learning*. London: Routledge/Falmer.

Knight, C. (2001) Chapter 4 in L. Abbot and C. Nutbrown, *Experiencing Reggio Emilia*. Buckingham: Open University Press.

Kress, G. (1982) *Learning to Write*. London: Routledge.

Laevers, F. (2000) Forward to basics! Deep-level learning and the experiential approach. *Early Years*, 2(2): 20–8.

Lindsay, G. and Desforges, M. (1998) *Baseline Assessment*. London: David Fulton Publishers.

McNamara, D. (1994) *Classroom Pedagogy and Primary Practice*. London: Routledge.

Malaguzzi, L. (1996) The right to environment, in T. Filppini and V. Vecchi (eds) *The Hundred Languages of Children: The Exhibit*. Reggio Emilia: Reggio Children.

Meade, A. and Cubey, P. (1995) *Thinking Children*. Wellington: New Zealand Council for Educational Research.

Meadows, S. (1993) *The Child as Thinker*. London: Routledge.

Merry, R. (1998) *Successful Children, Successful Teaching*. Buckingham: Open University Press.

Moyles, J. (1992) *Organising for Learning in the Primary Classroom*. Buckingham: Open University Press.

Moyles, J. (ed.) (1995) *Beginning Teaching, Beginning Learning*. Buckingham: Open University Press.

Moyles, J. (2001) Chapter 2 in J. Collins, K. Insley and J. Soler (eds) (2001) *Developing Pedagogy, Researching Practice*.

Nabuco, M. (1996) The effects of three early childhood curricula in Portugal on children's progress in the first year of primary school. University of London, London: PhD, Institute of Education.

Nabuco, M. and Sylva, K. (1995) Comparisons between ECERS ratings of individual pre-school centres and the results of Target Child Observations; do they match or do they differ? Paper presented at 5th European Conference on the Quality of Early Childhood Education, Paris.

NACCCE (National Advisory Committee on Creative and Cultural Education) (1999) *All Our Futures: Creativity, Culture and Education*. London: DfEE Publications.

NCC (National Curriculum Council) (1989a) *A Framework for the Primary Curriculum*. London: HMSO.

NCC (National Curriculum Council) (1989b) *A Curriculum for All*. London: HMSO.

NCC (National Curriculum Council) (1990) *The Whole Curriculum*. London: HMSO.

Norman, K. (1990) *Teaching Talking and Learning* in Key Stage One. York: National Curriculum Council.

Nutbrown, C. (1994) *Threads of Thinking*. London: Paul Chapman Publishing.

Nutbrown, C. (1999) *Threads of Thinking*. London: Paul Chapman Publishing.

Ofsted (1991) *Well-managed Classes in Primary Schools: Case Studies of Six Teachers*. London: HMSO.

Ofsted (1994) *Primary Matters*. London: HMSO.

Parker-Rees, R. (1997) The tale of a task: learning beyond the map, in A. Pollard, D. Thiessen and A. Filer, *Children and their Curriculum*. London: Falmer Press.

Piaget, J. (1959) *The Construction of Reality in the Child*. New York, NY: Basic Books.

Pointon, P. and Kershner, R. (2001) Organizing the primary classroom environment as a context for learning, in J. Collins, K. Insley and J. Soler (eds) *Developing Pedagogy, Researching Practice*. London: Paul Chapman Publishing.

Pollard, A. (1996) *An Introduction to Primary Education*. London: Cassell.

Pollard, A. (1997) *Reflective Teaching in the Primary School*. London: Cassell.

Pollard, A. and Bourne, J. (eds) (1994) *Teaching and Learning in the Primary School*. London: Routledge.

Ritchie, R. (1995) *Primary Design and Technology*. London: David Fulton Publishers.

Rogers, C. (1983) *Freedom to Learn for the 1980s*. Columbus, Ohio: Merrill.

Sainsbury, M. (1998) *Making Sense of Baseline Assessment*. London: Hodder and Stoughton.

Sammons, P., Hillman, J. and Mortimore, P. (1985) *Key Characteristics of Effective Schools*. London: HMSO.

Schweinhart, L. and Weikart, D. (1997) Lasting Differences. The High/Scope Preschool Curriculum Comparison Study Through Age 23. Monograph of the High/Scope Educational Research Foundation. Ypsilanti, Michigan: High/Scope Press.

Sotto, E. (1994) *When Teaching Becomes Learning*. London: Cassell.

Suschitzky, W. and Chapman, J. (1998) *Valued Children, Informed Teaching*. Buckingham: Open University Press.

Sylva, K. (1997) The quest for quality in the curriculum, in L. Schweinhart and D. Weikart, *Lasting Differences, Monographs of the High/Scope Educational Research Foundation Number Twelve*. Ypsilanti, Michigan: High/Scope Press.

Sylva, K. (1998) Early Childhood Education to Ensure a Fair Start for All. Lecture at RSA Handing on the Education Baton, 21 October.

Sylva, K. (2001) *Is Holistic Education Enough? Marianne Parry Lecture*. Lecture to Early Childhood Organisation (Bristol local branch).

Sylva, K. and Nabuco, M. (1996) Research on quality in the curriculum, *International Journal of Early Childhood*, 28(2): 1–6.

Temple, C., Nathan, R., Burris, N. and Temple, F. (1988) *The Beginnings of Writing.* Newton, MA: Allyn and Bacon.

Thompson, I. (1997) *Teaching and Learning Early Number.* Buckingham: Open University Press.

Tizard, B. and Hughes, M. (1984) *Young Children Learning.* London: Fontana Press.

Tizard, B., Burke, J., Farquar, C. and Plewia, I. (1988) *Young Children at School in the Inner City.* London: Lawrence Erlbaum Associates.

Trevarthen, C. (2000) Growing up with Confidence. Lecture at Chris Ollerenshaw Conference: Bath Spa University College.

Urquart, I. (2000) Chapter 9 in D. Whitebread (ed.) *The Psychology of Teaching and Learning.* London: Routledge/Falmer.

Valentine, M. (1999) *The Reggio Emilia Approach to Early Years Education.* Dundee: Scottish Consultative Council on the Curriculum.

Vecchi, V. (1998) The role of the Atelierista, in G. Ceppi and M. Zini (eds) (1998) *Children, Spaces and Relations: Metaproject for an Environment for Young Children.* Reggio Emilia: Reggio Children.

Vernon, M. (1971) *Human Motivation.* London: Cambridge University Press.

Vygotsky, L. (1978) *Mind in Society.* Cambridge, MA: Harvard University Press.

Webb, R. and Vulliamy, G. (1996) *Roles and Responsibilities in the Primary School.* Buckingham: Open University Press.

Wells, G. (1986) *The Meaning Makers.* London: Hodder and Stoughton.

Whitebread, D. (ed.) (1996) *Teaching and Learning in the Early Years.* London: Routledge.

Whitebread, D. (ed.) (2000) *The Psychology of Teaching and Learning.* London: Routledge/Falmer.

Whitehead, M. (1997) *Language and Literacy in the Early Years.* London: Paul Chapman Publishing.

Woods, P. and Jeffrey, B. (1996) *Teachable Moments. The Art of Teaching in the Primary School.* Buckingham: Open University Press.

Index